By the Letter

A COLLECTION OF SHORT PLAYS AND MORE

DAVID J. HOLCOMBE

ISBN 978-1-957582-20-7 (paperback)
ISBN 978-1-957582-21-4 (eBook)

Copyright © 2022 by David J. Holcombe

Cover design, "Rooftops of Prague" by David J. Holcombe

All rights reserved. No part of this publication may be reproduced, distributed, or transmitted in any form or by any means, including photocopying, recording, or other electronic or mechanical methods without the prior written permission of the publisher.

Printed in the United States of America

Contents

INTRODUCTION 1
ACKNOWLEDGEMENT AND DISCLAIMER 2
THE BECHAUT AFFAIR 4
THE BLACK PEARL 19
THE DISASTER CONTRACTOR 29
BY THE LETTER 38
A MOST TRUSTED COUNSELOR 52
REVOLVING DOOR 76
THAT'S LIFE 97
GOING TO ZAGREB 105
NOT TAKING THE SHOT 119
THE VIOLIN FESTIVAL 128
DETAILS, DETAILS, DETAILS! 138
A TRIP TO FULTON, LOUISIANA 150
DEFENESTRATION 159
COMMUNITY HEALTH 167
KATIA AND THE DEVIL 176
THE HOUSE ON SAVA STREET (PORTRAIT OF A FAMILY IN NINE HOLIDAYS) 184
WORLD WAR II REMEMBRANCES OF KENNETH G. HOLCOMBE AND VIRGINIA HARVEY HOLCOMBE 290
TWO SHORT STORIES 303

INTRODUCTION

Many of these plays deal with overt or hidden conflicts, whether in the work place or at home. Since some of them were written in the COVID era, there are references to that terrible pandemic which has taken more American lives than the historic Spanish Flu of 1918. The presence of face masks, while omnipresent in our difficult times, will seem like curiosities of another era to those who grow up in future, COVID-free times.

These works, like my extensive former writing, have remained almost unknown outside of a small circle of people in Central Louisiana. Since this, like my other works, is self-published, it might be dismissed as an enormous vanity project. Yet, while created in a very specific time, universal themes of fear, hope, greed, ambition and even love might raise them to a higher level.

It remains to future readers and even generations to discover what treasures lie hidden between these covers. Whatever you may or may not find among these pages, just remember that it represents the expression of an artistic soul, unmotivated by financial gain. As such, it is the clearest expression of the pure, indomitable creative spirit that can flourish even in the most unlikely locations.

ACKNOWLEDGEMENT AND DISCLAIMER

Many people have contributed to this volume, some intentionally and some unintentionally. All writers "write about what they know." Since a play should contain some conflict, and perhaps a completed dramatic arch, there will always be something familiar about the works. Conflict can be painful, but provides a rich terrain for the artistically inclined. Conflicts can be familial, professional or environmental. All bring in different characters and different settings, some of which may appear disturbingly familiar.

Despite similarities to the living (and perhaps dead), all of the plays are fictional. While some people may project themselves into the works, any resemblance to the living or dead is strictly coincidental. That being said, the world provides a constant parade of fascinating characters, some admirable, others revolting. The artist identifies those with the greatest dramatic potential and puts them on the page, and perhaps on the stage.

While COVID delayed work by our local developmental theatre group, Spectral Sisters Productions, we continued to limp along while waiting for better times. The elimination of staged performances during the pandemic has devasted theatres, big and small. It has, however, forced playwrights and other creative spirts to express themselves. The inspiration they took from these dreadful times will result in some astonishing works, specific for our pandemic age, but universal in the themes of isolation and social disruption.

So, oddly enough, I would like to acknowledge COVID-19 and our one-hundred-year pandemic which provided the subject matter for some plays (and scores of medical articles published elsewhere). The pandemic unleashed all sorts of reactions, both social and anti-social, which resulted in dramas on a local and national scale that continue to unfold. Crises bring out the best in some and the worst in others, and this pandemic has been no exception. That dichotomy will also be reflected in some of these works.

If you see yourself in any of the pages, just consider it your personal projection into the work, and enjoy the dramas portrayed. My apologies to anyone who might be offended, but, as William Shakespeare had Puck state:

"If we shadows have offended,
Think but this, and all is mended,
That you have but slumber'd here
While these visions did appear."

A Midsummer Night's Dream 5.1.440-455

THE BECHAUT AFFAIR

CHARACTERS

    PATRICIA: Middle-aged woman. Private banker. Casual dress.

    GEORGE: Younger middle-aged. Attorney-at-law. Casual dress.

    ROBERT: Middle-aged man. Sloppy dress. Patricia's brother.

SETTING

    Patricia's living room. They are seated around a coffee table and discussing business.

SCENE 1

PATRICIA: We can't do that!

GEORGE: Why not?

PATRICIA: Because it's a violation of fiduciary trust, that's why?

GEORGE: (*Stands and gesticulates*) Come on! This crazy old lady is sitting on several millions in cash, stocks and property. She doesn't have any close relatives except her retarded daughter. The other relatives are not close either emotionally or physically. (*Pauses*) We have to step in and protect their interests.

ROBERT: Their interests? Or yours.

PATRICIA: Ours, dear brother. You stand to benefit as much as I do, maybe more.

GEORGE: Precisely! So, we get old Mrs. Bechaut (*pronounced "Beko"*) to sign you up as her executor and me as her power of attorney and then we lock in the assets before anyone can object.

ROBERT: Anyone in their right mind knows that old lady is crazy as a loon. She's driven away all of her relatives with her paranoia and foul mouth. (*Pauses*) I certainly wouldn't want to be around her if I didn't have to be.

GEORGE: (*To PATRICIA*) You start on the financial papers and I'll start on the power of attorney documents. We can wrap this up in a week at most.

ROBERT: No court of law would recognize this. She would make a fool of herself before any judge. Anyone could see she's insane.

GEORGE: Incompetent is the word, not insane. Besides, if we have a signed affidavit from a well-respected doctor attesting to her sanity, we're home free. She's eccentric, not incompetent. You know what I mean. (*Pours himself another drink*) What some more?

PATRICIA: I'll pass.

ROBERT: You might find an obliging doctor, but you'll have trouble finding an obliging judge.

GEORGE: I can always find an obliging doctor and the judges around here are a bunch of cretins. Who are they going to believe, some respected local doctor or some out of town expert from the big city that the relatives might dig up? A local judge will go with the local doctor every time, trust me.

PATRICIA: What if they call Mrs. Bechaut to the stand.

GEORGE: Let them. (*Laughs*) She's so hostile, she'll read them all the riot act in a minute. Nothing crazy about that, just aggressive. Think of it, a poor little old lady, abandoned by her family until they smell the money slipping away into someone else's pockets. It would be a bunch of greedy, distant relatives pitted against some kind-hearted locals. Then the money slips right into our pockets (*puts his hands into his pockets.*)

ROBERT: Yes, yours, of course.

PATRICIA: No, ours! Wouldn't you want to live in that big house and be the care-taker while we get some sitters to deal with the old lady and her daughter. Nice furniture, Persian carpets, antiques and fine art. What's wrong with that?

ROBERT: It does sound nice, but who will own the house.

PATRICIA: Well, I will, eventually. We wait until the old lady dies and then we move the daughter into a group home until she dies.

GEORGE: It can't be long. The old lady is already sick and the daughter has got to have a shortened life expectancy, all retarded people do.

PATRICIA: Are you sure of that?

GEORGE: That's what our obliging local doctor told me.

PATRICIA: We get rid of the relatives early on, manage the money and then reap the profits as beneficiaries of the will, our will.

ROBERT: (*Points heavenward*) His will.

GEORGE and PATRICIA: Amen! (*Both laugh and take a drink.*)

GEORGE: To Mrs. Bechaut and her daughter!

PATRICIA: To her plentiful estate!

ROBERT: To her big, beautiful rent-free house.

ALL drink and set down their glasses.

ROBERT: What do you think that house is worth?

GEORGE: I'm no real-estate agent, but I'd estimate it at a half a million, not including the contents.

PATRICIA: That part of town is growing like crazy and it's a big piece of property, probably three acres or more, with a bunch of mature oak trees. It could be easily subdivided into luxury home sites or an apartment complex.

ROBERT: I can fire the current yard man and pocket that money as well, plus I can have the old lady buy a new riding lawn mower that I can use on the side for my own lawn business.

GEORGE: Good thinking.

PATRICIA: Which judge do you want to take the case?

GEORGE: I'd say Judge Swift. He's old, not too interested in details and very suspicious of outsiders.

PATRICIA: Sounds perfect.

ROBERT: Isn't he related to the old lady in some way? Everyone around here is related to everyone else.

GEORGE: I don't think so. Even if he were, he'd have to recuse himself at some point, which makes the whole process longer and more complicated.

PATRICIA: Don't we want this short and sweet?

GEORGE: Not necessarily. If we drag it out, it gets more and more expensive to the family who have less and less to gain. We can wear them down with motions and experts and delays of all sorts. I've played this game before and the outsiders always throw in the towel at some point. If they're already wealthy, which this family is, it's just not worth the hassle for them.

ROBERT: Especially if some local do-gooders get involved who are interested in the principle of thing, not just the money.

BY THE LETTER

GEORGE: (*Laughs*) Who are you talking about? Everyone's just interested in money. No one has principles when money's involved.

PATRICIA: I guess that goes for us, too?

GEORGE: Oh no! We're interested in protecting a vulnerable old lady and her handicapped daughter from abuse. Isn't that right?

PATRICIA: Of course!

GEORGE: And you, Robert, don't you agree?

ROBERT: Of course, we only have their best interests at heart. (*Pauses*) Just like taking candy from a baby.

GEORGE: (*To ROBERT*) That's not something we want anyone to hear. Don't be stupid and say stupid things or you'll kill the goose along with her golden eggs.

ROBERT: Can I do some remodeling of the house?

PATRICIA: Sure.

ROBERT: The kitchen is pretty shabby and old. Maybe some new marble counters and hardwood floor. I hate that green Formica.

PATRICIA: Sound's good to me. We're just helping to make the living environment better for both of them, and for us eventually.

ROBERT: And maybe a new car so I can chauffer them around.

GEORGE: Of course, but nothing too fancy. Maybe a Lexus or BMW.

ROBERT: I'd like that.

PATRICIA: And they'd like it too.

GEORGE: (*Serves some more drinks*) I propose another toast. To Mrs. Bechaut and her daughter!

ROBERT: And to the new kitchen and new floors and a new car and a new riding lawn mower.

PATRICIA: And to a new will with her private banker and private lawyer as beneficiaries to everything before and after their deaths.

ROBERT: And to their premature deaths (*pauses*) from natural causes.

GEORGE: Naturally.

PATRICIA: I'll start the paperwork tomorrow.

GEORGE: I'll get the power of attorney and medical power of attorney drawn up, signed and notarized by the end of the week. (*Drinks*) By the time her deadbeat relatives realize what's happened, it'll be a done deal. Let them sue us until the cows come home. They'll be so sick of the name of this town, they'll never want to come back or ever hear the sound of it again.

ROBERT: But how do I know you'll give me a share when the time comes?

GEORGE: A share? Won't you be living rent free with a caretaker's income for as long as they live? Isn't that enough? (*Pauses*) Besides, your sister here (*points to PATRICIA*), doesn't have any other relatives and you become her sole beneficiary in case she dies first. How about that?

PATRICIA: Hopefully, not too soon.

GEORGE: Of course, not too soon.

BY THE LETTER

ROBERT: I guess that sound's okay. It all depends on how long they live. If they don't live a long time, I'll get my money's worth. If not, it might be a bust.

PATRICIA: Long enough, but not too long. We could still run through the money if they live too long. Let's hope nature will take its course.

GEORGE: (*Raises his glass*) To nature's course.

PATRICIA and ROBERT: To nature's course.

BLACKOUT

SCENE 2

ROBERT, PATICIA and GEORGE are sitting in the same living room. It is 30 years later. There might be a change of decorative pillows or other minor changes. A bottle of whiskey is on the table with three glasses, already filled with drink. Everyone appears older, with white hair and slower movements.

GEORGE: How should I know that damn daughter was going to live another thirty years?

PATRICIA: None of us knew.

ROBERT: The old lady died pretty quick.

GEORGE: Ten years? I don't call that pretty quick.

PATRICIA: And that daughter, even with all her issues, just kept going and going and going. It's torture.

ROBERT: Not that much torture since both of you were getting your handsome honorarium paid, year after year.

GEORGE: True, but it still required effort. (*Pauses*) I thought everything might come unraveled when the old lady's will got challenged by her relatives and she had to testify, but it worked out okay.

BY THE LETTER

ROBERT: You were sweating it out with that fancy Dallas lawyer. He called you everything in the book, a sleazy, no good, abusive profiteer.

PATRICIA: Yeah, me too. But it didn't stick. Judge Swift just dismissed all of their objections and almost accused them of being out-of-town vultures, swooping in on a defenseless orphan. Some of the jury members were crying after he described the situation to them.

ROBERT: (*To GEORGE*) You did a fantastic job, too. That jury was convinced you were a saint, dedicated to the best interests of the late mother and retarded daughter. All those pictures of the beautiful house and yard, the daily menus, the physical therapy. They were eating out of your hand.

GEORGE: Just like the daughter used to do.

PATRICIA: Stop it! She didn't do that.

GEORGE: I saw it with my own eyes. You would feed her gummy bears out of the palm of your hand.

PATRICIA: That was toward the very end, when she had problems using utensils.

ROBERT: She almost nailed you, too, with the virus.

PATRICIA: How was I supposed to know her sitter brought COVID to her?

ROBERT: That's what the sitter died of, wasn't it?

PATRICIA: Yes, and it was almost what I died of, too.

GEORGE: Dedication to the bitter end.

ROBERT: A bitter end, indeed.

PATRICIA: How did I know that damn daughter was going to live that long and end up needing around-the-clock sitters for years. Who would have guessed she'd burn through all that money? No one could have known that.

GEORGE: Or that she'd get COVID and die and give the virus to you (*points to PATRICIA*) in the process.

PATRICIA: Precisely.

ROBERT: Maybe it was the hand of God, celestial revenge?

PATRICIA: You can be such a fool.

ROBERT: No, I'm serious. Maybe God was punishing you for taking advantage of a helpless old lady and her daughter.

GEORGE: Don't say things like that.

ROBERT: Isn't it true?

PATRICIA: And you, still living in her big house on that big property. You've done pretty well for yourself.

ROBERT: Your house, now. And what are you going to do with it? Live there? Let me continue to live there?

PATRICIA: Sell it, of course, as soon as I can.

GEORGE: I bet the value's gone up a lot.

ROBERT: You said the daughter ran out of money and that's why she had to go to that home with sitters.

PATRICIA: She did.

ROBERT: But she still had the house and the land. You could have sold that and gotten more money.

GEORGE: Thank God it didn't come to that. (*To PATRICIA*) At least we can divide that money up between the two of us. What with the yearly honorarium drying up, that will provide a few hundred thousand each I believe.

ROBERT: The two of you? What about me?

GEORGE: What about you? Rent free for thirty years, a steady income, a new truck, a new riding lawn mower. What else do you want? You didn't write the will or do the other paperwork. You didn't actually care for the old lady or the daughter. Why would you deserve any more? You already got more than you deserved.

PATRICIA: Enough! I'll talk to Robert later.

ROBERT: No, I think we need to talk now. I was in this from the beginning. I did everything I was supposed to do. I shut my mouth with the lawyers for the family and always defended both of you. That seems pretty important to me.

GEORGE: Is this blackmail? What exactly are you getting at here?

ROBERT: I could still go and denounce you both to the family and their lawyers. They could come after you both for everything you've got and throw you into prison to boot.

GEORGE: Throw US into prison (*makes and inclusive gesture*). You've been up to your neck in this scheme from the beginning. No one in their right mind would believe that you suddenly had a pang of conscience at this late date and wanted to do the right thing.

ROBERT: You don't know that.

PATRICIA: I think George is right. No one would believe you.

ROBERT: So, you'd turn against me, too.

PATRICIA: If you did something stupid like that, you bet your bottom dollar I would. I'd denounce you in a minute.

ROBERT: Sisterly love, eh?

PATRICIA: I'm not going to jail because you're a greedy little bastard.

ROBERT: Who's the greedy bastards here? You hatched this scheme. You worked it out. You benefited while you laughed all the way to the bank, month after month, year after year.

GEORGE: And you, too, you little shit. (*Advances and threatens ROBERT with his fist raised*) Just try and pull some crap like that and see what I'd do.

ROBERT: (*Grabs the nearly empty whiskey bottle and holds it up*) Touch me and I'll smash your brains out.

PATRICIA: (*Screams*) STOP IT!

ROBERT: (*Looks at her*) He started it.

> *As ROBERT looks at PATRICIA, GEORGE takes advantage of his inattention to smash ROBERT's face with his fist. ROBERT falls back, but gets up and lurches forward. As he does so, he breaks the bottle and uses the jagged edge to stab and slash GEORGE. GEORGE looks astonished, then grabs ROBERT by the neck and both fall to the ground. ROBERT lets the broken bottle drop and GEORGE seizes it and stabs ROBERT in the chest. Blood goes everywhere and ROBERT sinks back in death.*

BY THE LETTER

GEORGE: (*Stands up and lets the bottle fall*) He's dead.

PATRICIA: Are you sure? (*Knells down and check the pulse*) He's dead. We need to call 911.

GEORGE: Are you crazy? And say what exactly? That we had a domestic dispute and I killed your brother?

PATRICIA: We can't just walk away.

GEORGE: No, we can't. We are going to roll him into this carpet and go and bury him down by the bayou where the dirt isn't hard. (*Looks around*) We'll clean up this place and I can take his truck and drive it into the lake. That place is full of vehicles.

PATRICIA: Someone will start looking, start asking questions.

GEORGE: Will they? Who exactly? No wife, no kids, no other relatives besides you?

PATRICIA: But he's my brother.

GEORGE: Right! And we choose our friends, but not our relatives. Everyone knows that. He's been an ignorant pain in the ass the whole time. (*Points to the kitchen*) Now go and get those wipes. There's a ton of them in the kitchen. Bring them back and we'll start wiping up everything. All the clothes and pillows and the rug get thrown away or burned. This place has got to be spotless.

PATRICIA: I don't think I can do it.

GEORGE: (*Slaps her*) Now listen to me. You just finished stealing an old lady and her daughter blind. You drove away her family. You spent the money to pay off your house and now you're going to help clean up this mess and get rid of your brother. He was deadbeat and he was going to blackmail us to get the house or more.

PATRICIA: But his was my brother. He's all I have.

> *GEORGE shakes his head and turns to start cleaning up the mess. As his back is turned, PATRICIA picks up the broken bottle and jabs it into GEORGE's back. He turns in astonishment and she drives it into his neck. GEORGE stumbles back, clutching his neck.*

GEORGE: (*Gurgling*) You fucking bitch! (*Falls back onto ROBERT's body.*)

PATRICIA: (*Stands in the middle of the room and looks around at the bloody mess. Pulls a cellphone out and dials*) 911. (*Pauses*) There's been a terrible accident. Can you send an ambulance? (*Pauses*) 2020 Bayou de la Paix Road, the old Bechaut home. (*Lets the phone drop and sinks down onto the couch.*)

BLACKOUT

THE BLACK PEARL

CHARACTERS

    Leroy: Middle-aged Black man. Non-descript clothing.

    Marie: Middle-aged Black woman. Non-descript clothing

SETTING

    Leroy and Marie are in the cemetery on All Saints Day. There is a simple white cross and a few vases with flowers.

> *LEROY and MARIE are cleaning up the burial plot in the cemetery.*

LEROY: Okay, can we put the flowers out now or do we have to wait.

MARIE: We can do all the work now. That way, if other family members come by, they'll see we haven't forget Aunt Pearl.

LEROY: Right.

> *MARIE arranges some of the flowers and wipes some dirt off the simple white cross.*

MARIE: I think it looks really nice. She wanted to be buried here in the old cemetery, not in the new one. She likes the history of the place and some of her old relatives were already here.

LEROY: (*Pulling up some weeds between the stones*) What do you think about that man who wants us to sign a paper to print one of Pearl's plays?

MARIE: I don't really know. (*Pauses*) Is he just trying to make some money of her writing?

LEROY: He says it's just to keep her memory alive by putting her play in print with a bunch of plays by other local authors.

MARIE: It doesn't sound too bad, especially if it makes her famous. Maybe it's okay to do it.

LEROY: It might make her famous all right, and us too. I just don't know about that kind of fame.

MARIE: What do you mean? What does he want to print? Which play?

LEROY: "Hermaphrodite."

MARIE: (*Straightens up and scowls*) That weird play about the boy who starts to have his period and is half boy and half girl.

LEROY: That's the one.

MARIE: NO! That's out of the question. I'm not going to have my favorite aunt remembered for some pornographic play about boys having periods.

LEROY: It's not really about that.

MARIE: Then what's it about?

BY THE LETTER

LEROY: It's about children who are born different and the misery they have trying to establish their sexuality. (*Shows his right hand and then his left*) Are they a boy or a girl or both?

MARIE: That's not real, it's made up.

LEROY: No, it's real. She knew a boy up there on Cane River who had this happen to him. He started having his period at thirteen. It created quite the scandal up there.

MARIE: No! You're just making this all up.

LEROY: I am not! The kid was a normal appearing boy who had a slit behind the penis and that's where he peed and that's where the blood starting coming out. I swear to God. Aunt Pearl told me all about it.

MARIE: All the more reason not to let this man print that play. We'd be the laughing stock of the state. You'd ruin her reputation and ours. They already think we're a bunch of superstitious, ignorant peasants and perverts. It's just not normal or dignified.

> *LEROY and MARIE continue to tidy up the plot. LEROY puts a bottle of brandy on the cross.*

MARIE: That's not going to last too long around here. And it won't be the spirits that are drinking it.

LEROY: (*Shrugs*) It doesn't matter who drinks it. (*Pauses*) You know, Pearl's got quite a reputation as a writer, at least out West where she taught. But we locals don't have anything we're known for, except for being part of her family. Maybe we can just be a little bit famous because we let this man print her play.

MARIE: (*Stands up*) You're out of your mind! We never had anyone in our family who was a hermaphrodite. That's sick. It isn't natural. It's disgusting.

LEROY: Why? Kids don't choose to be that way. The kid she knew was just born that way and no one noticed he had a penis and a vagina until he started bleeding. Then he got all depressed because people thought he was cursed and could never have a normal life ever.

MARIE: Who was it?

LEROY: You probably didn't know him at the time. I think his name was Carter or Cantrell or something like that.

MARIE: What happened to him?

LEROY: He killed himself by jumping into the Cane River up around Cloutierville. It was really sad.

MARIE: If people thought he was cursed, then they should have been happy for themselves and for him when he died.

LEROY: Not really. (*Pauses*) Folks started to think that they had been too hard on him. And that a little bit of kindness might have made a difference. There are other folks like him out there in the world. He might have found someone like himself.

MARIE: Really? Two hermaphrodites living together? Who's the man and who's the woman and who'll have the babies. It's too disgusting to think about.

LEROY: So, I can't let the man print Pearl's play.

MARIE: Absolutely not!

BY THE LETTER

LEROY: (*Takes the bottle and opens it and drinks a swig of brandy*) I think we need to get this play published.

MARIE: NO! Get back to work. We've discussed it enough.

LEROY: Maybe. (*Takes another swig*) What if I told you that the boy didn't die.

MARIE: So?

LEROY: And what if I told you that I was that little boy. You still think it was sick and disgusting.

MARIE: (*Stands*) That's not funny!

LEROY: I'm telling you the truth. I'm the hermaphrodite. Aunt Pearl's favorite nephew. She was the only one I confided in back then. She was kind to me and understanding. She wrote about me.

MARIE: Stop this. It's not a joke (*starts to walk away*) and if it is, it's a bad one.

LEROY: No, it wasn't a joke then and it isn't now. You know how hard it was for me? Pearl was the only one who was kind to me when I started to bleed. I tell you, she never made fun of me or treated me any different from the other nieces and nephews. (*Goes and pulls her back*) Come back and sit down and finish cleaning up.

MARIE: (*Sits down*) Are you still bleeding every month?

LEROY: No, I think I hit menopauses.

MARIE: (*Laughs*) Menopause, eh? Men don't have menopause.

LEROY: If they're hermaphrodite, they do. I just got real irregular last year and then I stopped having periods altogether.

MARIE: (*Thinking*) That's why my tampons went so fast back then. I couldn't figure it out. They seemed to fly out of the package. You were using them too, weren't you?

LEROY: I had to get them somewhere and I couldn't exactly buy them in the store.

MARIE: (*Studies LEROY*) So, you were the hermaphrodite. I thought it was just a story, a made-up story about some made-up boy.

LEROY: No, it was based on reality. And I can tell you it was just as bad as what Pearl described. (*Pauses*) Was I a boy? Was I a girl? Was I both? Could I have sex? Babies? Get married? To a man? To a woman? It tortured me day and night.

MARIE: So, you decided to go with being a boy. I do declare! But the blood. And you got married and everything. Everyone thought you were just another normal guy.

LEROY: I kept it from my wife for twenty years. She left me finally, but not because of that. Not because of the bleeding or not having any kids, nor our bad sex life. (*Pauses*) It was when I found out I liked men, too. That was just too much. That was the end for her.

MARIE: What else have you been hiding from me? Hemaphrodite, bisexual, probably got AIDS and God knows what other diseases.

LEROY: No AIDS. I use PReP.

MARIE: What's that?

LEROY: HIV prophylaxis.

MARIE: Like a condom?

LEROY: (*Shakes his head*) No, just a pill each day.

BY THE LETTER

MARIE: I don't want to hear any more about that or hermaphrodites or anything else about this. We can't have this man publish this play. That's final! We'd have everyone in the family wondering who she was talking about. Somebody would ask you and you'd be stupid enough to say "oh yes, that was me." Everyone would know and we'd all just be the hermaphrodite's family.

LEROY: She was always telling her students to "write what you know." I just didn't know she was writing about me until a long time later. And then this man asks me to publish that play in a book. (*Pauses*) Maybe it's time we did let the world know. Maybe this'll make Pearl really famous. And I can stop hiding the truth from everyone in the family.

MARIE: Are you crazy? We'd be the laughing stock of this town. (*Pauses*) No, the whole parish, the whole state, the whole country! We know people from one end of this state to the other, as well as people all over the states. (*Pauses*) You may want people to know all of your dirty laundry, but I'll keep mine in the family, thank you.

LEROY: That's one way of looking at it, but the other is that Pearl will live on in a book. People may be reading her play for years to come, even generations to come.

MARIE: All the more reason that it dies with her and gets buried in this grave with her body.

LEROY: You cleaned out her house. Did you throw all of her writings away?

MARIE: No one wanted those old papers.

LEROY: The archivist at the university asked me about them, but I told him I didn't know what happened to them. He seemed really upset that maybe there were some important papers lying around and they might be lost forever.

MARIE: What's an archivist?

LEROY: Someone who collects old papers of historical or literary importance.

MARIE: Pearl published some things in some books, but she didn't publish any books herself, not that I knew about.

LEROY: She had a few plays they put on here in town some years ago. Did you go?

MARIE: Heck, no! I knew she could write some strange things, but this "Hermaphrodite" took the cake. And that's before I knew it was about someone in our family (*points to LEROY*), you.

LEROY: I saw the play, the hermaphrodite one. It was good. When I saw how the young man played me on the stage, it made me almost cry. It was like he really understood the problem and how the situation confused and scared him. I really felt sorry for the boy and wanted things to work out. Everyone in the audience felt that way.

MARIE: It's just play acting. No one cares about that. It's not real.

LEROY: But it is real. You saw the young man get all flustered when he first started bleeding. He was worried he was going to die. Then his friend, a neighbor girl figures it out. And instead of making fun of him, she helps him to deal with it. (*Pauses*) I really cared about the boy and the girl and what was going to happen to them.

MARIE: It isn't real. You can't really care about actors. They're just playing a part.

LEROY: But you do care. Pearl said that you had to make people in plays sympathetic or no one would care what happened to them.

MARIE: Another rule like "write what you know?"

BY THE LETTER

LEROY: Yeah, like that but "if you don't care about the people in the story or the play, then you don't care what happens to them." Pearl's second rule.

MARIE: Pearl was full of wisdom.

LEROY: Yes, she was full of pearls. So maybe we ought to let this man publish her play so other people can care about the people she writes about. They can care about me without even knowing me.

MARIE: You are something else. You just don't take no for an answer. (*Pauses*) Maybe it would be an honor to Pearl. Maybe we should give the man permission to publish something else. But not that play, for something else she wrote. I know she wrote a lot of other things, even other plays.

LEROY: I saw them, too. Some plays about voodoo and other subjects, but only the "Hemaphrodite" play struck my heart and made me feel my guts inside. It made me cry.

MARIE: Because you're one of them. Because she knew you and was writing about you. (*Pauses*) How many other hermaphrodites are out there in the whole state? One, two, maybe three at the most? It's really, really rare from what I hear. So, you let our family be humiliated so three people in the state can feel good about themselves? That's not a good calculation.

LEROY: Maybe yes, maybe no. Let's let posterity decide.

MARIE: Well, I don't agree and you'd better not let that man publish her play without my permission or there will be all hell to pay for you and for him. Is that what you want, trouble?

LEROY: No, I never wanted trouble, then or now. I wanted to have a regular life like everyone else. But you know that no one really has that. We all have some sort of weird bleeding, sometimes on the outside and sometimes on the inside, but we all have it. And it kills some people because they just aren't strong enough to accept it.

MARIE: And you are?

LEROY: I am.

MARIE: (*Gives LEROY a hug*) I'm proud of you. I still love you and so did Pearl, but you can't publish that play. It goes to the grave with her. (*Pauses*) If you want to write your own play about your life, go ahead. That's your prerogative. You can take full responsibility, just like you did for your own bleeding. And if you want to talk about your wife and your boyfriends and HIV and whatever, just go right ahead. But leave me and the rest of the family out. We have enough worries and problems. (*Pauses*) Give me your word.

LEROY: (*Looks heavenward*) Aunt Pearl, I feel like I'm betraying you, but (*to MARIE*) I'll give you my word. Hermaphrodite will remain unpublished.

MARIE: Good! Now let's make sure everything looks perfect around here. I want it to be spic and span for All Saints Day. Pearl might be looking down on us now and God knows what she's thinking.

LEROY: I think I know. Here's to you Aunt Pearl (*takes another swig from the bottle and puts it down*). (*Looks heavenward*) Thanks, Pearl. I did my best, but I can't convince the living any more than talk to the dead. Forgive me. We both did our best. We all do, I guess.

MARIE and LEROY exit the cemetery.

BLACKOUT

THE DISASTER CONTRACTOR

CHARACTERS

    PATRICK: Middle-aged man with modest pot-belly. Wears a N95 mask.

    REBECCA: Younger middle-aged women. Wears a blue, surgical mask.

    DYLAN: Young middle-aged physician. (Wears a N95 mask and a stethoscope around his neck.

SETTING

    An austere set with a few folding chairs and a table. There are a couple of cots on the set as well. Nothing attractive on the walls.

        PATRICK, REBECCA and DYLAN are seated in folding chairs and working on and off on their laptops. The all wear masks, either surgical or N-95 masks.

PATRICK: I'm sorry, but we just can't accept this level of sloppiness about mask wearing and social distancing.

REBECCA: We're all wearing our mask.

PATRICK: Yes, those flimsy surgical masks that won't even stop a droplet.

DYLAN: That's not true. They're fine, just not quite as good as a N-95.

PATRICK: Not quite as good! That surprises me coming from a doctor, especially one employed by us. You should know better than that. We were all fit-tested for our N-95s to make sure they work. (*Points to REBECCA*) Those surgical masks are almost a joke.

DYLAN: A joke? All that fit-testing is the joke. (*Pauses*) It's a bunch of play-acting to make everyone think they'll get protected.

PATRICK: Not much respect for science from a doctor. You always surprise me.

DYLAN: Sometimes I surprise myself.

PATRICK: Speaking for surprises, I was surprised when your boss (*turning to REBECCA*) gave that insulting orientation. She denigrated us after ten minutes and just wouldn't stop.

REBECCA: That's not true. She said we could help you do a better mission. And she said you shouldn't come in here and say, "I'm here to help, now get out of the way."

PATRICK: That's not our intention. Besides, we certainly don't believe that she has anything to offer us. Starting off by treating us like dirt is not the way to achieve cooperation.

REBECCA: You are supposed to be here under our command. It doesn't sound like that's your understanding of the situation.

PATRICK: Because it's not! Violating our chain of command, confusing the staff with conflicting orders, questioning our judgement, refusing to put basic safety measures into practice, that's not helpful. It's dangerous and destructive and I won't stand for it.

DYLAN: Aren't we working for them? Aren't they paying for us to help them?

PATRICK: We're paid to accomplish a mission. If I can't have my staff work under safe conditions, then there won't be a mission.

REBECCA: The mission remains if you accomplish it or not. It's just we don't have the resources, so your services are being enlisted to do what we can't accomplish with our limited personnel.

PATRICK: Precisely, you're inadequate and we're here to help, not the contrary.

DYLAN: Can we talk about the bathrooms again?

PATRICK: We should. They're filthy and our staff has to use the same bathrooms as the patients. That's unacceptable.

REBECCA: Can you rent your own port-a-potties and put them outside?

PATRICK: That's not in our contract.

REBECCA: Then what's the solution?

DYLAN: Why don't we just close off part of the toilets and use the other entrance for our personnel. That way we can reserve a section for our employees and the rest of the bathrooms can be for the shelterees.

PATRICK: Can we do that?

REBECCA: I don't see why not. (*Pauses*) That was easy. Now, what's the next issue.

PATRICK: Our staff can't go back to their hotels because there is no electricity or hot water there, so they need to stay here. They'll need a section of the building to sleep in, one with better cots and no proximity to the shelterees.

DYLAN: But this is a shelter. It's for evacuees, not us. Don't they get priority.

REBECCA: It's a 200,000 square foot building. I suspect we can find a suitable place for your staff.

PATRICK: Of course you can. And I suggest the very furthest corner where it's a lot quieter.

DYLAN: But our staff will have to walk all the way there through the shelteree areas. Is that safe in a pandemic?

REBECCA: (*To PATRICK*) He's right. That puts everyone in danger.

PATRICK: Danger! Why aren't all these shelterees getting tested?

REBECCA: There aren't enough tests. Besides, there's a constant coming and going among the shelterees and we'd have to test them over and over again. This isn't a prison, so they're free to come and go.

DYLAN: They're COVID testing the folks in the medical section. No one has been positive so far.

PATRICK: A miracle. (*Stops and answers his phone*) Yes, Patrick speaking. We'll be done in a minute. And I won't be at the unified command meeting. I've got more important things to do. (*Pauses*) Of course there are more important things. We have some sort of medical emergency with a worker.

DYLAN: Shouldn't I know about that. I'm the doctor.

PATRICK: Yes, go over and check her out. One of our workers is seizing and they may need to go to the hospital.

BY THE LETTER

DYLAN get up and exits.

REBECCA: Is that the lady taking big doses of Keppra®?

PATRICK: How do you know about this?

REBECCA: Because I was talking to her and she mentioned that she was taking a huge dose of seizure medication and hoped she wouldn't have one. She was worried it might be provoked by the stress and the long hours on deployment.

PATRICK: Well, apparently it was.

REBECCA: Is it safe for someone like that to come out on a mission?

PATRICK: Of course, all of our workers are medically screened.

REBECCA: By who?

PATRICK: Our Medical Director.

REBECCA: I belong to a Disaster Medical Assistance Team and they won't clear anyone who might be a liability to the mission.

PATRICK: Are you challenging the integrity and judgement of our Medical Director?

REBECCA: I don't even know him. I was just sharing my experience.

PATRICK: You sound just like your boss. I guess the apples don't fall far from the tree.

REBECCA: My boss says that any group's leadership sets the moral tone for the organization and that tone is adopted by all of the subordinates.

PATRICK: Is that supposed to be a criticism of our group?

REBECCA: No, just a quotation.

> *DYLAN returns and comes to pick up his laptop.*

PATRICK: Well?

DYLAN: No exactly sure it was a seizure. She's going to need to go to the emergency room for a Keppra® level.

PATRICK: (*Looks around*) This damn place doesn't have any lab work.

REBECCA: Glucose finger stick, pulse oximeter and urine dip sticks.

PATRICK: Yes, field medicine at its best.

REBECCA: It's a shelter, not a hospital.

PATRICK: No labs, no x-rays, and a handful of medications. Nothing, in fact.

REBECCA: We got you a lot of donated medications from the Free Clinic, that's been helpful.

PATRICK: After a week of begging and pleading. (*Pauses*) How do you expect us to work under these sorts of conditions?

DYLAN: We're supposed to be here to assist as best we can. Everyone here's been impacted by the storm. (*Pauses*) I think the locals have been helpful and pleasant.

PATRICK: We'll have to agree to disagree. Being really helpful means working to make the conditions acceptable in order to accomplish the mission.

BY THE LETTER

REBECCA: To accomplish the terms of your contract for which you are being paid millions.

PATRICK: And worth every penny of it.

DYLAN: And you accuse Rebecca's boss of arrogance?

PATRICK: (*To DYLAN*) You are being handsomely paid to come here and work with us. That does not include insubordination and insults. We get enough of that from this young lady's boss (*points at REBECCA*).

REBECCA: I appreciate and admire my boss. She works very hard to hold our group together and never makes us do anything she wouldn't do herself. She tries to work with everyone of good will and we have run this shelter again and again without a single death. That's not bad. Plus, she's a decent person who looks out for the best interest of the people of this state, including her employees.

DYLAN: Quite a testimonial.

PATRICK: (*To DYLAN*) Isn't it your turn now?

DYLAN: Turn to do what?

PATRICK: To lavish praise on your boss. (*Stands up and points to himself*) That's your cue.

DYLAN: Eh. . . . (*stammers and falls silent*).

PATRICK: (*Looks between DYLAN and REBECCA*) Maybe we have a little something going on here? A little complicity? A field deployment romance? Is that what's happening here?

DYLAN: Of course not!

PATRICK: Then where's my praise?

DYLAN: You don't want praise in your presence. That's just flattery. (*Pauses*) You know what La Fontaine said about that.

PATRICK: The fountain? No, I don't know who that is our what they said.

DYLAN: "*Tout flatteur vit au depens de celui que l'écoute.*"

PATRICK: Okay, smart ass, what is that supposed to me. I don't speak whatever language that is.

REBECCA: I know! It's French and means "All flatterers live at the expense of he who listens to them."

DYLAN: Very good. How come you speak French?

REBECCA: I minored in French in college. We had to memorize that poem, "*Le Renard et le Courbeau*," in class (*Pauses*) and this is Louisiana, after all.

PATRICK: Don't remind me.

DYLAN: Come on, that's insulting.

REBECCA: I don't care. (*To DYLAN*) You have not stopped ranting and raving about my boss and her insulting rhetoric and it's all just projection and a reflection of your personal insecurity.

DYLAN: Wow, this is getting intense!

PATRICK: I've had enough. This place is a danger to my physical and mental health and I need to get out of here.

DYLAN: Do you need a medical certificate?

PATRICK: Maybe, but not from you.

BY THE LETTER

PATRICK grabs his laptop and walks out.

REBECCA: Well, that solved one problem.

DYLAN: You really are something. Are you married?

REBECCA: Divorced.

DYLAN: Engaged?

REBECCA: (*Sighs*) Yes, in fact I am.

DYLAN: Anyone I know?

REBECCA: Yes.

DYLAN: Who?

REBECCA: My boss. She's a real keeper.

DYLAN: Can you have an office romance like that, I mean really like that?

REBECCA: Of course, this isn't the Old South anymore. When we get married, I'll have to change departments. You can't directly supervise one of your relatives.

DYLAN: Makes sense. (*Pauses*) I wish you the best of luck.

REBECCA: You, too.

BLACKOUT

BY THE LETTER

CHARACTER

    DR. PETER SINGER: Royal Health Officer

    BEATRIX: Older woman, slightly obese, head of Royal Medical Operations

    CARLA: Young middle-aged woman (works at Royal Medical Operations)

SETTING

    Non-descript office building with several chairs and a table. King's portrait.

DR. SINGER: Insubordination, that's all it is! Dr. Sheppard defied the King's orders and she has to pay for it, that's all. The only question is how much.

BEATRIX: Dr. Sheppard swears she made the decision, not to pre-empt the King, but to conserve resources that were in eminent danger of waste.

DR. SINGER: Yes, she said that, but it doesn't matter. She had ample opportunity to discuss the matter with me or you or anyone. Dr. Sheppard just chose not to do it.

BY THE LETTER

CARLA: What's the real issue here? That there was an error in judgement or that someone got blindsided?

DR. SINGER: Blindsided! You're damn right someone got blindsided, the King and me. We had to learn about her unilateral proclamation in the newspaper. One territory was doing something different than the others. I had to hear how I was unable to control my own personnel and if I wanted to keep my head, someone had to pay.

BEATRIX: I thought you already called her.

DR. SINGER: You bet your ass I did. I called in the middle of the night and explained the gravity of her blunder and told her there would be immediate consequences: confiscation of medical supplies, reversal of her suggested policy changes accompanied by a public declaration of guilt and restrictions of her media access effective immediately.

CARLA: Media access restrictions? I thought she was one of the media stars of the ministry. Everyone says so?

BEATRIX: You can't say anything you want anytime to the media.

CARLA: Even if it is the truth?

DR. SINGER: Who cares about the truth? It's the public perception that matters. It's the King's perception that matters. And if everyone thinks there's being unequal distribution of resources and that some territories aren't getting what they deserve, that's a public relations problem for the Crown.

BEATRIX: Especially when the legislators get involved.

DR. SINGER: Precisely! Someone even suggesting that there is inequality or inequity in the system which makes the King and all of us look bad. Let investigative reporters find out these things if they can, but not through our own ministerial personnel. It's outrageous.

CARLA: It did result in some ministerial scrutiny and some changes.

DR. SINGER: Changes need to come from the top, not from the bottom and certainly not from the poorest, sickest, least educated part of the kingdom as a by-product of thoughtless interviews by the territorial medical officer.

BEATRIX: So, what do we do now, a disciplinary action?

DR. SINGER: Yes, a disciplinary letter, a really strong one with a threat of removal if there are any more transgressions.

BEATRIX: Three strikes and you're out?

DR. SINGER: Yes.

CARLA: What are the other two strikes?

BEATRIX: First, inciting the press to hone in on the inequality and inequities between territories.

CARLA: That's one.

BEATRIX: Then her blatant disregard of royal directives by unilaterally changing policy.

CARLA: I thought Dr. Sheppard told you (*to DR. SINGER*) that it was a temporary expedient to conserve resources, not a policy change.

BEATRIX: (*To CARLA*) You fool! If the King views it as a policy decision, then it was a policy decision. It Dr. Singer views it as a selfish blunder, then it is a selfish blunder.

DR. SINGER: Yes, that's good. Three strikes and you're out. (*To BEATRIX*) You're good at this, I know you do it all the time. Type something up right how and print it up afterwards.

BY THE LETTER

BEATRIX goes to a laptop and begins typing. DR. SINGER and CARLA continue to talk.

CARLA: I do feel sorry for her. Dr. Sheppard's one of the best loved and respected medical supervisors among all the territories.

DR. SINGER: And the most foolish.

CLARA: I'm not sure she's a fool. (*Pauses*) Don't you think this was perhaps an overreaction?

DR. SINGER: NO! If anything, it's an underreaction. Dr. Sheppard should be terminated on the spot for her insubordination.

CLARA: Doesn't insubordination mean willful disobedience? Sounds like she just wanted to get rid of perishable medical supplies in a timely way. Sounds like more of a *faux pas* than insubordination.

DR. SINGER: *Faux pas*, indeed! I was blindsided, the King's authority and mine were undermined by her behavior. It's intolerable! This is the minimum punishment, not the maximum. She needs public humiliation, confiscation of resources and strict surveillance with any media, just as I requested, as well as this disciplinary letter. Maybe that will finally get her attention.

CLARA: This seems harsh for someone who has devoted years of her life to the people of her territory. We get nothing but praise from citizens and politicians and the military about her leadership. Don't you worry that this will only enhance her stature?

DR. SINGER: Who's side are you on, anyway? You realize that defending the indefensible is the surest way to the exit. Her actions were sinful and stupid, even if you are personally sympathetic to her. This is government, not charity. This is power, not a parlor game.

BEATRIX: How about this? (*Reads*) "Dr. Sheppard: This memo serves as formal notice of disciplinary action resulting from insubordination and blatant disregard of directives from Royal Health Ministry leadership. Your actions were egregious and without defense."

DR. SINGER: Good start, go on.

BEATRIX: "By unilaterally deciding to disregard the King's eligibility criteria (outside of eminent resource waste) you jeopardized the confidence in this critical mission to ensure medical coverage among priority vulnerable groups as set forth by the King. That action was wrong and detrimental both for the Ministry of Health team and particularly for those 70+ territorial residents still working hard to get much-needed medical attention."

CLARA: I thought Dr. Sheppard already removed the ineligible citizens and replaced them with people who were aligned with the King's directive? I thought she did that as soon as she was told.

DR. SINGER: She did, the very same night as our conversation. But her actions still reeked of insubordination and punishment must follow. Whether her errors were acknowledged and corrected is irrelevant. (*To BEATRIX*) Go on.

BEATRIX: (*Continues reading*). "Broadcasting this to the media without any internal Royal Ministry of Health discussion was wrong. And, your silence in not notifying Royal Ministry of Health's leadership and instead having them find out about this from the media was wrong, and not the mark of a good team member."

DR. SINGER: Good, very good. I love your style.

CLARA: So, the real sin wasn't so-called insubordination, but having the Ministry of Health be blindsided by a public announcement, like I said before.

BY THE LETTER

DR. SINGER: NO! Being blindsided is an inconvenience, and a manifestation of insubordination on her part. Usurping the King's authority was the real sin. You cannot outshine the King. (*To BEATRIX*) Go on!

BEATRIX: "Such behavior suggests a disregard for your role as part of the Royal Ministry of Health kingdom-wide team and undermines the teamwork and organizational structure necessary for success across a large system. This is a formal warning, and the final warning. Good teams cannot excel with players who play only for themselves. Similar behavior in the future will result in separation from the Royal Ministry of Health team. Beatrix Requin, Supervisor of Clinical Operations for the Royal Ministry of Health."

DR. SINGER: I like it. A formal and final warning, just what we need in her supervisory file to proceed to immediate dismissal if necessary. (*To BEATRIX*) You're really a genius.

BEATRIX: No, just a faithful servant of the King and yourself, Dr. Singer.

CLARA: Lots of teamwork language in the letter, but is that the reality?

DR. SINGER: What do you mean?

CLARA: I understand that Dr. Sheppard has created a very impressive and competent team in her territory. They have regularly achieved and exceeded our goals and have gone above and beyond in any number of initiatives. There appears to be a real team at the territorial level.

BEATRIX: And we don't have a team?

CLARA: Of course, we do, at the kingdom level in the capital. We work very well together. But how much real interactions do we have with the territories? We tell them what to do, we issue directives, we make demands, but do we really consider their input in any meaningful way?

It's more like there are two parallel teams, one the territorial level and another for us at the Royal Health level.

DR. SINGER: That sounds seditious.

CLARA: Just playing the devil's advocate.

DR. SINGER: Well, the devil's advocate might burn in the fires of my anger and you'll be cast into hell with the real devil, our nemesis, Dr. Sheppard.

CLARA: That sounds like a threat.

DR. SINGER: No, it doesn't sound like one, it is one! Pick your sides carefully. You can be a territorial advocate and support Dr. Sheppard, but you must always retain complete authority over territorial personnel. And you must be completely subservient to me, and the King, of course. If you don't comply you'll be cast out with the trash. (*To BEATRIX*) It's Friday, isn't it?

BEATRIX: Yes, sir.

DR. SINGER: Present this letter to her today at 4 p.m. via zoom and you both must be present. That's the usual day and hour of royal executions, isn't it?

BEATRIX: Yes, traditionally it is. No scenes in the middle of the day in the middle of the week. It's worked well over the years. Friday afternoon executions. I've had a lot of experience.

DR. SINGER: Remember, you must both be there. You act as witnesses to one another and it adds to the intimidation factor. You both know the drill.

CLARA: I'm a bit concerned. Dr. Sheppard is a very honest and forthright person. She'll surely say she was concerned about resources and did not willfully disregard the King's directives. She'll say she wanted to avoid eminent waste in accordance with Royal degrees.

DR. SINGER: Who cares what she says? I've already heard it all before from her lips. You just deliver the message.

BEATRIX: Dr. Sheppard has also shown a propensity to defend others from unreasonable attacks from the ministry. As Clara mentioned, she has also had a decades long track record of exemplary achievements. She'll surely bring it up.

DR. SINGER: Let her. That was yesterday and this is today. This is about a transgression, which wipes away all past meritorious behavior. We cannot and will not tolerate insubordination. All the territorial medical directors must understand that. And if it takes making this one an example, then so be it. Sometimes you just need a sacrificial lamb, a scape goat. (*Pauses*) If her actions go unpunished, then what's next, voting on policy decisions? Truly incorporating the territorial concerns into the decision-making process? Creating a real team at the Health Ministry level with true territorial input? (*Pauses*) NO! That's all unacceptable.

CLARA: My other concern is that she's independently wealthy. She doesn't depend on her salary or pension for her long-term financial security. She comes from distinguished minor nobility and could leave at any time.

DR. SINGER: So much the better! She steps out of line again, we fire her and her pension disappears. It may not send her to the poor house but it certainly sends a message to those less fortunate in our service.

CLARA: That seems so punitive.

DR. SINGER: It IS punitive. All of this is punitive. By the way, the King's going to change his directives in three days to align with those Dr. Sheppard suggested, so none of this is even necessary from a policy standpoint. Dr. Sheppard jumped the gun. You can't do that. You can't pre-empt the King.

BEATRIX: That sounds like a personal vendetta.

DR. SINGER: Shut up! Both of you. This is not personal, it's political, the politics of survival. And I intend to be the survivor even if I have to sacrifice someone from around this place. (*Looks at BEATRIX and CLARA*) That goes for any insubordinate medical director or anyone in this office, including both of you. Do I make myself understood?

CLARA and BEATRIX: Yes, sir!

DR. SINGER: PERFECTLY CLEAR!

CLARA and BEATRIX: YES, SIR!

DR. SINGER: I have a meeting with the Royal Council. I have to go. Carry on!

> *DR. SINGER exits leaving BEATRIX and CLARA alone in the room.*

CLARA: (*Sighs*) Well, that was intense.

BEATRIX: So will the discussion with Dr. Sheppard. You can guarantee it.

CLARA: I don't know. She's a reasonable person.

BEATRIX: Yes, being treated unreasonably, but who cares. (*Pauses*) I hate doctors. I hate them all. They're insufferably pompous, arrogant, self-centered and entitled bastards.

CLARA: That's harsh.

BY THE LETTER

BEATRIX: But justified. They cause me more heartburn than any other part of this job.

CLARA: You mean Dr. Singer?

BEATRIX: He's actually easier to deal with than some others, like Dr. Sheppard. At least Dr. Singer is a high-level political appointee. They come, they go, but we remain. They may sit on the throne, but we are the power behind the throne. (*Stands and walks around the room*) You smile, you say "yes sir" and "no sir" or "yes ma'am" and "no ma'am." And then you wait and watch as the gears of the state grind them down and spit them out. (*Pauses*) They're stuck between the political vultures above and the sharks below.

CLARA: Who are the sharks?

BEATRIX: What a fool! I thought you were a smart woman. We're the sharks. We are the silent prowling crowd of civil servants who circle around, waiting for an arm or a leg to dangle down so we can chomp with impunity.

CLARA: I don't believe that.

BEATRIX: You don't? Well, you're not going to last long around here. (*Picks up her letter*) This letter is full of teamwork this and teamwork that. There is a team and it's us. We are the team, the group that counts, the ones that support each other to advance in the royal hierarchy. A raise here, a promotion there, and you have a tidy sum to contribute to your retirement. It's not about the people, it's not about the damn medical directors or the Royal physician, it's about us, first, last and always.

CLARA: It's kind of depressing.

BEATRIX: No, it's life in the bureaucratic state. We just have to survive the Dr. Singers and the Dr. Sheppards, the good ones and the bad ones who come and go. And we pick up the pieces if and when they tear themselves apart.

CLARA: You think Dr. Sheppard will tear Dr. Singer apart?

BEATRIX: (*Laughs*) Don't I wish. But she's too nice and too noble for that. Dr. Sheppard will make us feel guilty about doing our job (*swings the paper around*), writing a nasty, humiliating letter. But it won't work. I'm incapable of guilt and you should be, too.

CLARA: Is there no way to be moral in this business.

BEATRIX: No, none! It's about survival and using your wits to avoid the pitfalls and the landmines. That's where Dr. Sheppard's a fool. She really cares about the people and she believes in the basic goodness of mankind. That kind of person sometimes makes it through life thanks to their sheer emotional idiocy.

CLARA: She's no idiot. She has several degrees and speaks several languages. She can't be an idiot.

BEATRIX: She's book smart, but totally naïve to the world. She'll be totally blindsided by this letter (*holds up the paper*) and Dr. Singer will get his revenge. But it will be short lived.

CLARA: Why?

BEATRIX: Because he's attacking a wonderful medical director who is beloved by her territory. She's lived there for decades and everyone knows her. She's slaved to get resources there and actually cares about poor people and forgotten racial groups. This is a big and diverse kingdom, you know, with lots of ethnic groups and she loves them all.

CLARA: Yes, I know. And her territory is the poorest, sickest and least educated as she reminds us all the time.

BY THE LETTER

BEATRIX: She should shut her mouth.

CLARA: But it's the truth.

BEATRIX: Who cares about the truth! Championing the poor and downtrodden either citizens or co-workers will generate some temporary buzz, but get you screwed in the end.

CLARA: Or crucified.

BEATRIX: Precisely! You're learning.

CLARA: (*Pauses*) Dr. Sheppard may claim she's serving at the King's discretion and only he may fire her at any time with a phone call. Isn't that true?

BEATRIX: Of course not! She's serves at the discretion of the administration.

CLARA: Who's that exactly?

BEATRIX: (*Points to herself*) Me, of course!

CLARA: Not the Royal Health Officer or the Health Minister?

BEATRIX: Of course not. The one's only an foolish doctor and the other is a transient political appointee. They come and go like the seasons. (*Pauses*) No, it comes down to me, the true power behind the throne.

CLARA: And if she appeals directly to the King?

BEATRIX: (*Laughs*) Let her try! "*L'état, c'est moi,*" remember. It'll go nowhere.

CLARA: Aren't you worried that your professional judgement might be clouded by your personal animosity to Dr. Sheppard?

BEATRIX: NEVER! Nothing clouds my professional judgement. (*Looks at her watch*) It's about time we made this call to Dr. Sheppard. Are you ready?

CLARA: As ready as I can be.

BEATRIX: NO! You have to be completely ready. Do not respond to or listen to any of her argumentation. If she calls this management by humiliation, or reminds us of her services to the Royal Health Ministry or her territory, you just ignore it and move on. You're a witness so we can report back any inappropriate language or behavior. That would be more fuel on the fire for Dr. Singer's rage. Ready?

CLARA: Okay. Let's do it.

BEATRIX: (*Pauses and eyes CLARA*) I'll take you out to dinner afterwards. I know a little place that's pestilence free, clean and not too expensive. We'll have a great organic meal, a good bottle of wine and who knows what happens after that.

CLARA: I'm very tired and we haven't even started the conversation with Dr. Sheppard. That will be exhausting, I can already feel it.

BEATRIX: Clara, this is not an invitation you can refuse. People have tried that in the past and they are no longer with us. You work for me, get my drift?

CLARA: Yes, loud and clear.

BEATRIX: So, let's zoom Dr. Sheppard and get this unpleasantness out of the way.

CLARA: And what if she appeals to the local politicians or the general public?

BY THE LETTER

BEATRIX: She won't dare. If you thought Dr. Singer was enraged before, he would be ballistic if Dr. Sheppard dared do anything like that. She's not going to the locals or to the King, trust me.

CLARA: So, she has no moves left except submission and humiliation. She just needs to learn to live in constant fear like the rest of us.

BEATRIX: That's right, total submission and humiliation.

CLARA: Dr. Sheppard might surprise us. She doesn't seem to have any healthy fear of authority or speaking her mind.

BEATRIX: She'll be afraid, alright, when we get through with her. (*Pauses*) Let's go. I'm ready to get this out of the way and go get dinner. At least this encounter should be amusing. I'm starving.

CLARA: Like a shark circling its victim?

BEATRIX: (*Laughs*) Yes, exactly, just like a hungry shark.

> *BEATRIX and CLARA gather up some papers and leave the room. BEATRIX grabs CLARA's arum and gives it a little nibble. CLARA pulls away at first and then allows the gesture to continue. The music to "Little Shark" or perhaps the theme to "JAWS" plays as they exit.*
>
> **BLACKOUT**

A MOST TRUSTED COUNSELOR

CHARACTERS

> SULTAN: Older man with an imperious manner.
>
> COURT PHYSICIAN: Middle-aged man.
>
> GRAND VIZIER: A sly fellow with a sense of his own survival.
>
> SULTANESS: Beautiful and alluring.

SETTING

> Court of the Sultan. Minimal set elements. A golden throne and a gaudy scepter. There is a floor to ceiling window on one side of the stage with French doors that open up.

SCENE I

PHYSICIAN: You Highness, it's a pestilence, no doubt about it.

SULTAN: Does it kill people?

PHYSICIAN: Yes, especially the old and infirm and those of the poorer classes.

VIZIER: Is that necessarily a bad thing? After all, the elderly are non-productive citizens and the poor pay no taxes. No potential taxes, no *raison d'être*. Perhaps it's better if this pestilence just takes its natural course and kills them off. Kill two birds with one stone, so to speak.

PHYSICIAN: That's immoral, of course, but also dangerous. The old ones live with their younger family members and they'll not all die. Some require great care and monopolize the energy and resources of their families and our hospitals. The poor are already incapable of taking care of themselves. They'll all end up in the hospitals by droves. That's a huge drain on medical resources.

VIZIER: Perhaps.

SULTAN: How is this disease transmitted?

PHYSICIAN: Much is unknown, since this came from the East, but it appears that it jumps from person to person when they are in close contact.

SULTAN: Not by the water or tainted food?

PHYSICIAN: It appears not.

PHYSICIAN: How did it get here?

VIZIER: I'm told that it came with merchants from the East, from your natural enemies.

SULTAN: We still trade with those enemies and their goods go through our lands to people in the west with much profit for our merchants. I see no good in making them a scapegoat. I'm sure they didn't invent this sickness.

VIZIER: They may well have invented it and sent sick people into our lands to weaken your rule. It's certainly possible, if not probable, Your Highness.

SULTAN: (*To VIZIER*) That doesn't solve the current problem. (*To PHYSICIAN*) What do we do now?

PHYSICIAN: We should close the city to prevent further spread to other parts of your lands and we should isolate those who are ill from others to prevent contagion. We should avoid gatherings, cancel all sporting events and religious services and mandate face coverings to prevent person-to-person transmission.

SULTAN: But that would paralyze our city and plunge the economy into ruin. There would be starvation and riots.

PHYSICIAN: You have ample grain, water and wine for months in case of siege. This is a siege of an invisible enemy.

VIZIER: Face coverings? Like a hijab?

PHYSICIAN: Precisely, but covering the face, not just the hair and for both men and women.

SULTAN: Ridiculous! I'd look like a fool, like a woman. No self-respecting ruler would wrap their face in public. It's not becoming for a sultan.

PHYSICIAN: You'd be leading your people by example, Your Highness, a true leader in sickness and health, a role model for the incredulous.

SULTAN: (*To PHYSICIAN*) Enough! Leave us now but remain in the palace so we can speak later. I must consult with the Vizier.

PHYSICIAN bows and exits.

SULTAN (CONT): (*To VIZIER*) What do you think about all of this? Could he be telling the truth or does he have some sinister motives?

VIZIER: Your Highness, there's indeed a pestilence, but I believe your physician overstates the seriousness of the illness. He also underestimates the catastrophic effects on your economy. (*Pauses*) Such drastic measures would cripple commerce in the city and between the capital and the provinces, not to mention between surrounding kingdoms. Your treasury would suffer as would your royal standing.

SULTAN: But if we don't shut down, then we could have hundreds, perhaps thousands of deaths. Would I not be blamed for such a slaughter? Putting profits before people?

VIZIER: Won't you be blamed when the people are starving in their houses with no money, no jobs and no source of income? (*Pauses*) You've brought them unparalleled prosperity. Your people sing your praises as you lift up the economy and put them to work. Even the poor have jobs now and they look to you to continue their upward mobility.

SULTAN: What if the physician is right? What if we lose both the country's health and its prosperity. What then?

VIZIER: What then! You continue to rule and you promise them a return to prosperity in the future, however distant that might be.

SULTAN: You're right. I should suppress all news of this illness and make it a crime to speak of it. That'll reassure the people and we can continue as before. See no evil, hear no evil, speak no evil.

VIZIER: And the physician?

SULTAN: He'll be asked to remain silent. If he's asked his opinion by the nobles or merchants, he must defer to me and I'll be the bearer of good news, not bad news. I must remain the optimistic voice of the kingdom, the people's Sultan. The Royal Physician will be supervised at all times, or silenced if necessary. I'll be the voice for the people.

VIZIER: Indeed, you should.

SULTANESS enters.

SULTANESS: My Lord. May I have word?

VIZIER: Should I retire?

SULTANESS: No, it isn't necessary. (*Continues to SULTAN*) I've heard tell of a terrible illness that ravages the people. It strikes the old and wreaks havoc among the poor people in the city slums.

SULTAN: Who told you this? The physician?

SULTANESS: No, I have heard it whispered among my servants and the ladies of waiting. They've seen it in their families and among their friends.

BY THE LETTER

SULTAN: What do they say?

SULTANESS: They say the disease jumps from one household to the next and from one person to the next on the wind. First there's a high fever and then a terrible cough. After that, the person either gets better, or continues to worsen until they're gasping for breath and often die.

VIZIER: Surely these are exaggerations of simple minds.

SULTANESS: No, these are both from the house staff and the nobility. They've all seen and heard of it, but death stalks the slums more than anyplace else. The poor are stricken down by the hundreds. Everyone is afraid.

SULTAN: What do they expect? I cannot invite everyone into the safety of the palace.

SULTANESS: No, but they want you to close the city gates to protect from more disease from travelers and distribute food and water from the Royal Storehouse.

VIZIER: We've discussed that, Your Highness, and that would deplete the reserves and leave you open to naked aggression from your enemies. Besides, the threat of this disease has been largely exaggerated. You must project strength and fortitude, courage and determination.

SULTAN: By cowering in my palace and ignoring the moans of the public?

VIZIER: The public must be dominated. If there are riots, crush them. If there is rebellion, exterminate it. You are the power. You are the authority. You are the sultan.

SULTANESS: You are also the shepard of the people. They look to you in their time of distress.

VIZIER: (*To the SULTAN*): Any sign of weakness will be misinterpreted, Your Highness. You'll have open opposition not only among the little people, but in the nobility. They're the pillar of your power, along with the army, of course.

SULTAN: (*Sighs*) I have heard it said that no ruler rules but by the silent consent of the governed. If that's true, then the consent of my people still remains important.

VIZIER: Interesting, but incorrect, Your Highness. With all due respect, fear, a strong military and the support of the ruling class keeps you on your throne. It has also been said that it is better to be feared then loved as a ruler.

SULTAN: Perhaps. (*Pauses*) Bring back the Royal Physician.

> *VIZIER bows, then goes out and brings back the PHYSICIAN.*

PHYSICIAN: (*Bows to the SULTAN*) At your service.

SULTAN: I consider you a trusted counselor, along with the Vizier. What do you think I should do?

PHYSICIAN: Close the gates to keep more infection from coming in and keep those in the city from spreading it around the countryside.

SULTAN: What else?

PHYSICIAN: Keep the people confined to their homes. Provide them food and water for their survival. And wait.

SULTAN: How long?

PHYSICIAN: I cannot tell you. This is a new illness and its course remains uncertain. What I can tell you with certainty is that it kills your people, especially the old ones, and it cannot be treated. They live or they die. When enough are infected, it will leave like it came. But many will die before that time. For the rest, I can only answer with uncertainty.

SULTAN: Uncertainty? How can I rule with uncertainty? I need facts. I need figures. I need predictability.

PHYSICIAN: No one but God know the answers.

VIZIER: And the soothsayers? We can get some to read the stars or animal guts or tea leaves.

PHYSICIAN: Rubbish. (*Pauses*) I can give you a count of the daily dead and their ages. With that we can surely see if the disease increases or declines.

VIZIER: Giving such woeful data to Your Highness will only frighten him and inflame the people. (*To PHYSICIAN*) If you have such numbers, they must come to me at the palace and no place else. Don't you agree, Your Highness?

SULTAN: Perhaps we should know among ourselves first, then decide the best route. Until then, the gates remain open and the people must be allowed to move about. We will pretend that this illness doesn't exist. That is my order.

SCENE II

Same setting. A few weeks later.

SULTAN: (*Holding his nose*) What is that awful odor?

VIZIER: That's the smell of burning bodies, Your Highness.

SULTAN: Burning bodies?

VIZIER: Yes, your troops are burning piles of dead on the outskirts of the town. The cemetery is full and the bodies are being dumped in the streets.

SULTAN: Why not just expand the cemetery? Dig more graves? Create more space?

VIZIER: It's not possible. Even if they land was available, there aren't enough men to dig the graves. As it is, they just dig an immense hole and pile the bodies on wood and burn them. It's ghastly work, but many want to do it because it pays well and few other jobs exist. Then they pile more wood and more bodies on the ashes and start over.

SULTAN: By whose orders is this happening?

VIZIER: The Royal Physician ordered it. (*Pauses*) He said it was a measure of public safety, like closing the gates and confining the public.

SULTAN: Who's in charge here? Me or the Royal Physician?

BY THE LETTER

VIZIER: For matters of government, you are in charge. But for matters of health, you have deferred to him.

SULTAN: Summon him at once!

> *VIZIER bows and goes to get the PHYSICIAN. Both re-entry and bow to the SULTAN.*

VIZIER and PHYSICIAN: Your Highness.

SULTAN: What's the meaning of this foul odor.

PHYSICIAN: It is foul, Your Highness, but the health of your people demands it. The bodies were being left in the streets to rot. Flies and rats proliferate and pestilence fills the air and the streets. Putrid liquids run off into the gutters and foul the wells.

SULTAN: Did you ask my permission to do this?

PHYSICIAN: No, but I have done it in the public interest as you have commanded me to do. (*Pauses*) Would you want me to stop?

SULTAN: No! Do what is best for the people. (*Pauses*) How many have died?

PHYSICIAN: An exact count is unknown, but there have been tens of thousands already.

SULTAN: (*Shocked*) It was only a few thousand a few weeks ago.

PHYSICIAN: Yes, but the disease has spread from the slums to the houses of the well-to-do. It spares no one, rich or poor, old or young, powerful or meek.

SULTAN: (*Pulls back*) It's not in the palace, is it?

VIZIER: Oh no! We check all the servants and the bureaucrats every day to make sure they have no signs of disease. Anyone with any signs, or coming from a household with anyone who is sick is escorted out immediately.

PHYSICIAN: To my knowledge, there have been no cases, but there are so many people in the palace, it would be a miracle to have no one enter who was not infected. (*Pauses*) Even when we screen each person for fever, there are many who are infected who have no symptoms at all, at least in the beginning of the illness.

SULTAN: (*To PHYSICIAN*) That is your responsibility to determine anyone who is ill, however difficult that may be. (*To VIZIER*) And your responsibility to make sure they are removed.

VIZIER and PHYSICIAN: (*Both bow*) Yes, Your Highness.

SULTAN: Where is my wife?

VIZIER: In her chamber. I'll summon her here.

> *VIZIER exits and returns with the SULTANESS. Both bow to the SULTAN.*

SULTANESS: Your Highness, what can I do for you?

SULTAN: Have any of your servants told you of disease in their families?

SULTANESS: No, but everyone knows of a family who has suffered loss. The disease strikes entire households: children, parents and grandparents alike. Some live, but many die an atrocious death, gasping for air and going mad with fever. No amount of water quenches their thirst. Bringing them to the hospital only fills the beds, overwhelms the physicians and serves no useful function.

SULTAN: (*To PHYSICIAN*) Is there no cure?

BY THE LETTER

PHYSICIAN: None that has worked. We have tried herbs and spices and various liquors and concoctions of wholesome and unwholesome objects. Nothing works. A lucky few survive and they seem to be protected in some mysterious way from the disease. But many die.

SULTAN: Your job is not just to burn bodies, it is to also find a cure. You need to seek out every famous doctor, every possible remedy, try everything that even promises a cure.

PHYSICIAN: We have reached out to all the surrounding empires and all have suffered the same fate. No one has yet found a cure, although many have been proposed by charlatans, thieves and fools. Sometimes the supposed cure is deadlier than the disease. (*Pauses*) I have an obligation to protect the public.

SULTAN: (*Screams*) YOU HAVE AN OBLIGATION TO PROTECT ME AND MY FAMILY. (*Grabs his wife*). If she dies, if my child dies, you will die, too, Royal Physician, make no mistake about it.

PHYSICIAN: I will do my best. Sometimes the forces of nature and the will of God are stronger than the will of men.

SULTAN: FOOL! I have absolute power. I tell the people to build a wall, they build a wall. I tell me army to conquer this kingdom or that, and they do it. I tell you to protect my family from death, you will do it, too. (*Pauses*) Physicians are as plentiful as fish in the sea, but Sultans are unique gifts of God. (*Looks heavenward*) And the will of God and the Sultan become one.

>*Shouting is heard from the street. The VIZIER and the SULTANESS go and look.*

SULTAN: What is it?

VIZIER: The people are rioting.

SULTAN: For what?

SULTANESS: There is not enough food or clean water. They have no money and no jobs. Death stalks every door. And the city gates are closed so they cannot even escape to the countryside.

SULTAN: And spread the disease to every corner of the sultanate? (*To PHYSICIAN*) Isn't that what you said?

PHYSICIAN: Yes, it it's true. There will be no part of your sultanate untouched. Plus your city will be a ghost town, with only the dead left.

VIZIER: Well, at least the dead don't riot.

SULTAN: (*To VIZIER*) Send out troops and put an end to this disorder. I command it.

SULTANESS: Why add to the slaughter and inflame the situations, My Lord? Hasn't there been enough death and destruction in the city already?

SULTAN: (*Raises his hand to strike the SULTANESS*) How dare you contradict me! I raised you from nothing to be the first woman of the Sultanate.

PHYSICIAN: (*Steps in and puts his arm up to protect the SULTANESS*) Please, Your Highness, your wife is beloved of the people renowned for her compassion. She's only looking out for your welfare and theirs.

SULTAN: (*Strikes the PHYSICAN who falls to the ground*) Miserable traitor! (*To VIZIER*) Look at these two! They work behind my back to undermine my authority.

SULTANESS: (*Leans down to comfort the physician. Speaks to SULTAN*) He only looks out for your good and the good of the people. He's an honest man. A good man.

BY THE LETTER

SULTAN: AND I AM NOT?

> *SULTAN kicks the SULTANESS who sprawls out next to the PHYSICIAN. The SULTANESS screams from pain and clutches her side. The PHYSICAN moans. The VIZIER looks on impassively.*

SULTAN (CONT.): (*To VIZIER*) Escort them out. Lock them in the dungeon. Get the troops out in the street and squelch this rioting however you can. (*Goes and sits on his throne*) I will not tolerate this disobedience. There is rebellion in my own palace and on the streets. It must stop and it will stop.

SCENE III

Same setting a few weeks later. The lighting is somber.

> *The SULTAN, wrapped in a crimson robe, is sitting on his throne. The VIZIER enter with the SULTANESS who is in dressed in rags.*

SULTANESS: (*Bows to the SULTAN*) Your Highness.

SULTAN: Come here. Let me see you.

SULTANESS: (*Approaches with her head bowed*) You wishes are my commands.

SULTAN: The dark and the dank of the dungeon do not suit you. Your complexion has faded like a fine flower in the dark. And your clothes reek of urine and excrement. You've lost a lot of weight. Do they not feed you?

SULTANESS: I give my food to the other prisoners and I care for an older woman who has lost control of her bladder and bowel. There's no one else to care for her.

SULTAN: What did this woman do?

SULTANESS: She approached the palace with a crowd that was shouting for food and shelter.

BY THE LETTER

SULTAN: Ah, a rebel.

SULTANESS: No, a loyal citizen with four starving children since her husband died of the disease.

VIZIER: I'm sure there's more to the story, Your Highness.

SULTAN: And the physician, your friend, how does he fare?

SULTANESS: I don't know. Men and women prisoners are held separately.

VIZIER: He's in solitary confinement per your instructions.

SULTAN: Fetch him here. Let's see if solitary confinement has worn away some of his pretention.

SULTANESS: He only acts in the best interest of Your Highness and the people.

SULTAN: He solved no problem! He let this disease destroy my kingdom, decimate the people, obliterate our prosperity. You call that my best interest?

SULTANESS: No man could hold back this illness any more than they could hold back the tide.

SULTAN: Such insolence is intolerable. (*To the PHYSICIAN*) Do you agree with her? Can I not undo this illness and prevent it, just with my God-given authority?

PHYSICIAN: I believe you know the answer to that as well as I do. Is there any need for me to speak?

SULTAN: (To VIZIER) And you, Vizier, what say you? Do I have the authority and the power?

VIZIER: (*Bows low*) I'm here to serve Your Highness and not to delineate your powers.

SULTAN: (*Goes and grabs the SULTANESS and gives her his cloak*) Here, take my cloak and cover your filthy garment.

> *The SULTANESS puts on the cloak and allows herself to be taken by the SULTAN.*

SULTAN (CONT): Remember when we danced in the moonlight in the garden. (*Begins to dance with the SULTANESS*) Your beauty enchanted me.

> *The waltz music from Kismet plays and the SULTAN and SULTANESS dance for a minute until the music fades. They stop and the sounds of screaming come from outside the window.*

SULTAN (CONT): (*To the PHYSICAN*) You hear them shouting in the streets. (*Pulls the PHYSICIAN to a window which flickers the torchlight*) You see them, fighting with the palace guards.

PHYSICIAN: I see the scene.

SULTAN: What do you think I should do?

PHYSICIAN: Continue to isolate the city, but give enough food and water so that everyone can stay in their homes until the illness begins to pass away. Share some of your vast wealth. Show them you care. As you, yourself have said, "no ruler rules but by the silent consent of the governed."

VIZIER: It has also been said that it is better to feared than loved, remember.

BY THE LETTER

SULTAN: (*To PHYSICIAN*) Somehow, this was your fault. Somehow you let this foreign disease into my kingdom. And somehow your counsel has led into more disease, more chaos and more death. You should have foreseen this illness and prevented it before it ravaged my kingdom.

SULTANESS: It's not his fault, Your Highness, it's the will of God.

SULTAN: (To SULTANESS) Shut up!

SULTAN: (*Takes the PHYISCIAN by the shoulder and points out the window*) That is what your learned advice has brought upon us and someone has to pay. (*SULTAN grabs the PHYSICIAN and shoves him out of the window.*)

SULTANESS: (*Screams*) NO! (*Rushes to the window but stops at the edge.*)

SULTAN: Not ready to follow you lover into the abyss, my dear? Perhaps you need a little push to join him?

VIZIER: (*Steps forward*) I do not think that would be advisable, Your Highness. The people love you wife and her death would only inflame them. I think she's been loyal to you. Perhaps her death would be the spark that brings down the throne.

SULTAN: You, too? Is there no one I can trust? (*Rampages around the palace as he moans and tears his clothing*). To be brought down by an infection? Is it possible? With all my troops, power and wealth, I cannot stop an invisible enemy that destroys my kingdom?

VIZIER: We still have time. There are still other strategies. You could flee to the mountains and wait out the illness. It would give me time to restore order in your absence. Let them hate me, Your Highness, not you.

SULTAN: Do you think the mob would tear me limb from limb if they get inside the palace? The troops have been decimated with disease. There's not one guard in ten who has not been infected. There is no line of defense. (*Pauses*) Yes, perhaps I should flee. Things will be better by winter. (*To VIZIER*) Get my baggage ready. Prepare a special guard to escort me from the palace and out through the city gates.

VIZIER: It shall be done. (*To SULTAN*) And your wife? What is to become of her?

SULTAN: (*To SULTANESS*) Will you come with me, even disgraced as you are? I'm sure there will be a spare room somewhere.

SULTANESS: No, Your Highness, my place is here with my people. I can work in a hospital or turn the palace into one. My first duty is to you, but since I am disgraced, my second duty is to those who suffer. Let the will of God be done.

SULTAN: What foolish blather. (*To VIZIER*) Make sure that the royal treasure comes with me. Choose a few loyal nobles to serve me as an honor guard. Take whatever remains of the royal guard and turn them into my escort. Keep a few guards to defend the palace from the mob (*exuts the room with a flourish*).

SCENE IV

Same palace. A few days later. There is a muted light coming in through the window. The VIZIER sits on the throne while the SULTANESS is making bandages.

VIZIER: Quiet, isn't it?

SULTANESS: Yes, Your Excellency. (*Pauses*) And what news of the Sultan? Is he safely in his mountain refuge?

VIZIER: Oh, him? No, I'm afraid not.

SULTANESS: What do you mean? He's not safe in the mountains?

VIZIER: No, he's dead.

SULTANESS: (*Stands up and drops what she is working on*) WHAT?

VIZIER: Yes, you heard me. He's dead. He didn't make it too far from the city when the royal guard killed him. It appears that it all happened very quickly.

SULTANESS: How can you be so certain?

VIZIER: Oh, I'm certain all right. The head of the royal guards came back and reported the whole affair. Not only was the Sultan killed, but most of his loyal nobles as well.

SULTANESS: How did it happen? Why did it happen?

VIZIER: Because I ordered it.

SULTANESS: You ordered it?

VIZIER: Yes! (*Pauses*) Surely you didn't think I would miss this opportunity to take the power that I've so long desired.

SULTANESS: I don't believe you.

VIZIER: Well, you should. (*Pauses*) Never let a good crisis go to waste. Since your son died of the disease, there was no legal heir. You could not inherit the throne and I was the logical choice. (*Pauses*) If only the Sultan were out of the way. (*Pauses*) When he decided to flee, it was my perfect opportunity.

SULTANESS: But the people? Do they know? Why don't they rise up? They'll never accept you.

VIZIER: (*Plays with the scepter*) *Au contraire*, lovely lady. We announced that the Sultan had committed suicide over his failure of leadership. (*Pauses*) With the food stores open and the city gates re-opened, there was no one left to object. I also gave a portion of the royal treasury to the people. Not all, of course, just enough to make them think that I cared. (*Pauses*) I also let them out of confinement by opening the city gates.

SULTANESS: Disease will spill out into the countryside. It will also come spilling in with refugees and merchants. It will never end.

VIZIER: Yes, it will end as all infections end. We will learn to live with it.

SULTANESS: The Royal Physician did not think so.

VIZIER: He's dead, remember? And the people still miss him, God bless his soul (*looks heavenward and clasps his hands*).

BY THE LETTER

SULTANESS: And what other lies have you told the people?

VIZIER: Funny you should ask. I also announced that the very popular Sultaness, yourself, of course, has graciously decided to become my wife. That way the legitimacy of the throne is established.

SULTANESS: NEVER!

VIZIER: Never? I think not. (*Pauses*) I have always been attracted to you, both physically and intellectually. With my pragmatism and your compassion, we can make an unbeatable team, not to mention beautiful children.

SULTANESS: You're mad! You've killed your ruler. What would it take for you to dispose of me when my usefulness runs out and my beauty fades?

VIZIER: Nothing. Nothing at all. In fact, you've condemned yourself in your own words. (*Pauses*) That being said, nothing prevents us from enjoying a few years together until I tire of you. There are any number of women in the kingdom just dying to take your place.

SULTANESS: Many are already dead, thanks to you and your bad advice.

VIZIER: I only sought to please your husband, fool that he was.

SULTANESS: A fool, perhaps, but not an evil person.

VIZIER: Evil? I'll show you evil.

> *The VIZIER rises and begins whipping the SULTANESS who falls to the floor. He continues to kick her as she whimpers and tries to protect her face.*

SULTANESS: STOP! For the love of God. I'm pregnant.

VIZIER: (*Laughs out loud*) Well, I'll be darned. You harbor a legitimate heir to the throne. All the more reason to continue (*continues to kick the screaming SULTANESS*).

> *Cheering comes from the street. The VIZIER stops and approaches the window. He looks down at the crowd and spreads his arms. The crowd roars louder.*

VIZIER: (*Without turning he speaks to the SULTANESS*) You see, they adore me already. And they'll adore you, too, once we've taken care of that creature inside you.

SULTANESS: (*Rises painfully to her feet and runs to the window*) No! We'll die together (*throws herself out the window.*)

> *Horrified screams, gasps and murmurs from the crowd. The VIZIER looks startled and then regains his composure. Goes to the window.*

VIZIER: My people! The Sultaness, God receive her soul, was driven mad by the death of her husband and her only child. I proposed to take her as my bride, but grief overcame her. By this act, however, the start of a new reign begins. Food, wine and water will be yours as long as they last. This terrible disease will become a distant memory. We'll build a new, brighter future together.

> *The crowd screams "Vizier, Vizier, Vizier" which gradually transforms into "Sultan, Sultan, Sultan."*

VIZIER: I hear your voices and will accept the heavy burden of power. Together, we'll make this empire great again.

CROWD: (*Screams*) Yes! Yes! Yes!

BY THE LETTER

VIZIER: Yes, make the empire great again!

> *The crowd continues to chant "SULTAN, SULTAN, SULTAN!"*

VIZIER: Thank you, my citizens. A new day is dawning! No more talk of pestilence and death. Those days are already behind us. We will speak of them no more. A glorious future lies ahead. Let's go to it at once.

> *The crowd continues to chant "SULTAN, SULTAN, SULTAN!" The light from the window veers to blood red and then fades to dark.*

BLACK OUT

REVOLVING DOOR

CHARACTERS

> DR. ADAM BRIGHT: Younger middle-aged man, articulate and sensitive
>
> CHRISTINA BRIGHT: Dr. Bright's wife. Younger middle-aged, articulate and attractive.
>
> BEATRIX REQUIN: Civil Servant. Older middle-aged woman.
>
> ANTHONY LAFLEUR: Elected official. Marked Southern accent

SETTING

> Stage right in the Bright home. Nothing fancy. A couch and coffee table. Stage left is an official office with a desk and chair. There should be an American flag and a portrait of the Governor.

SCENE I

CHRISTINA and ADAM are in their home. CHRISTINA is sitting and ADAM walks around while he talks on his cell phone. He hangs up and sighs.

CHRISTINA: You can't go on like this. It's killing you and destroying our family.

ADAM: There isn't a lot of flexibility. We're going through a crisis that requires 110% of my time. You know that as well as I do.

CHRISTINA: No one has 110% of their time. And your family is certainly not getting anywhere near 50%. You come home exhausted. You answer phone calls all evening and all the time on weekends. You wake up at 4:30 worrying about everything. You're at the Governor's beck and call days, nights, weekends and holidays.

ADAM: That's my job. That's what they pay me for.

CHRISTINA: Don't be ridiculous. You were told you could achieve a work-life balance and they would be sensitive to your family's needs. What a crock of crap!

ADAM: No use being vulgar. It doesn't help and it doesn't make you sound very cultivated, which I know you are.

CHRISTINA: Well, all my cultivated qualities are gone. I'm reduced to a bitter spouse, groveling for scraps of left-over time from you. (*Hands ADAM an empty glass*) Get your own drink.

ADAM: (*Goes and gets a drink*) Would you be happy if I quit?

CHRISTINA: Yes, I would.

ADAM: Even in the middle of a state crisis?

CHRISTINA: I don't care about the state. I care about you and our family.

ADAM: You know that leaving would reflect poorly on me professionally.

CHRISTINA: You have an established reputation and this hell-hole job will not enhance your C.V. in the least.

ADAM: It still makes me feel bad for my colleagues.

CHRISTINA: What colleagues?

ADAM: My professional colleagues at the bureau.

CHRISTINA: Those were your employees, not your so-called colleagues. And they certainly weren't your friends.

ADAM: Some tried.

CHRISTINA: Yeah, by over burdening you with work, after hour calls and extra projects and then holding you to impossible timelines?

ADAM: They all worked as hard as I did.

CHRISTINA: For goodness sake, they're long-time civil servants with their jobs and pensions to worry about. Every one of those people knows exactly what they are going to earn and when they can retire. And they know how much their latest salary increase will benefit them. Plus, they can calculate their sick leave and regular leave bonuses to the exact hour and their anticipated extra income, too.

ADAM: Some do.

CHRISTINA: You can be so naïve. You're just a pawn in their game, a temporary place-holder while they feather their nests. How many people have been in your position in the past 10 years? Do you know? Do you care?

ADAM: I heard from one person that I've been the tenth in 15 years.

CHRISTINA: That makes a tenure of 1.5 years for an "important" position.

ADAM: There's got to be a good explanation.

CHRISTINA: Yes, it's a position with lots of visibility and no authority. (*Pauses*) Who would want a person there who can actually accomplish something? Change threatens people and you were just a temporary impediment to their agendas, whatever they are.

ADAM: I had moral authority. Everyone recognized my moral integrity and compassion.

CHRISTINA: Yes, it's true, but they put you in an unwinnable position. People calling you day and night to be here and there. You go to a press conference, to a meeting, to a legislative session, to an advisory council. Plus, you get raked over the coals by a bunch of reactionary politicians. All the while, you neglect your family, destroy your health and accomplish nothing. What kind of a job is that? (*Pauses*) You're too good and too smart to stay here.

ADAM: I have accomplished some things and I don't want to leave in the middle of a crisis.

CHRISTINA: The crisis is here *(swings her arms around)* in your own home and in your own family. For goodness sake, they'll be some temporary head-shaking and some critics, but all those people will weep and wail and convert you into some sort of saint when you leave, then move on to the next sacrificial lamb.

ADAM: You can be so cynical. When did you become that way?

CHRISTINA: Watching you kill yourself in a job conceived to fail.

ADAM: *(Takes CHRISTINA in his arms)* I know you care about me and I care about you, but I also care about those people. There are good people at work, dedicated people. I just can't figure out how to satisfy everyone.

CHRISTINA: *(Pushes him away)* Then don't! It's government. It will continue to function with or without you. That army of civil servants will keep grinding along with the same relentlessness whether you are there or not.

ADAM: I thought I could help with providing a caring moral compass.

CHRISTINA: And I'm sure some of your colleagues recognized that and will sorely miss you. But you cannot sacrifice yourself on the altar of the state. They may convert you to sainthood, but martyrdom shouldn't be required.

ADAM: It's happened before.

CHRISTINA: Yes, and Jesus rose from the dead. But it won't happen to you.

ADAM: Ah yes, mortal aims befit mortal men, as the Greeks said.

BY THE LETTER

CHRISTINA: Exactly. (*Pauses*) Did you want to hear about your son's experience in school today?

ADAM: (*Sighs and sits down*) Of course.

CHRISTINA: He came home crying because he got treated as a pussy.

ADAM: What!

CHRISTINA: Yes, he repeated something he heard us say about white supremacy or gay rights or something he overheard at the dinner table. And when he repeated it a school, a kid called him a pussy.

ADAM: What does "pussy" have to do with anything.

CHRISTINA: Who knows? Kids are just cruel.

ADAM: I thought that was a good school with a bunch of liberal folks, black and white, gay and straight.

CHRISTINA: It is. But there's a thin veneer on civilization here. You can't whitewash 300 years of prejudice, even in a liberal city.

ADAM: What did you do?

CHRISTINA: I reported it to the principal who said that such behavior is not a reflection of the values of the school and she would talk to the other student and his parents.

ADAM: That's good, isn't it?

CHRISTINA: Yes, except that the kid's father is some politician and a big donor to the school. Not promising, eh?

ADAM: I can talk to the dad.

CHRISTINA: Of course, you can't. You're a public servant and you told me yourself you can't reach out to legislators of any kind without permission from the administration.

ADAM: Maybe it is time to leave this state.

CHRISTINA: There are lots of opportunities elsewhere.

ADAM: Yes, but somehow, they all come with the same liabilities.

CHRISTINA: I don't believe it. There's got to be something less stressful and better supported. Just ask how many people have been in the position prior to you. If it's dozens, like here, then just don't go there unless the potential experience compensates the risk taking.

ADAM: I have learned a lot here. Some good things, some bad things.

CHRISTINA: Like what?

ADAM: Like that you can find decent people anywhere and they respond to kindness and compassion with reciprocity.

CHRISTINA: Like you wife? And your son?

ADAM: Of course.

CHRISTINA: Remember, a job is just a job. It's not a vocation. If the family is your number one priority like you say, than you have to realize you can't continue with what you are doing and have it both ways.

ADAM: Maybe I can negotiate some changes?

CHRISTINA: You can try, but good luck. (*Pauses*) Who exactly are you going to talk to? Your boss? The governor? Your subordinates? Who actually decides? There is no government, just the people that make it up.

ADAM: There are policies and job descriptions. (*Pauses*) Let me start with my boss and see where that goes.

CHRISTINA: (*Goes over and brushes ADAM's hair*) Go to bed. It's late and you're not going to solve this tonight. And try and sleep all night for once. Waking up at four in the morning isn't helpful. You're just exhausted.

ADAM: I agree.

ADAM and CHRISTINA exit.

SCENE II

ADAM enters the office and BEATRIX rises to greet him. Both are wearing surgical masks.

BEATRIX: Hello.

ADAM: (*Comes over and gives BEATRIX an elbow rub then retreats and pulls a chair to a safe distance*) How are you doing? Can I sit down?

BEATRIX: Sure. (*Sits down*) What can I do for you?

ADAM: You know how hard I've been working.

BEATRIX: Of course. This has been a particularly challenging time. So many problems and so many needs. You're pulled in twenty directions.

ADAM: Precisely.

BEATRIX: And you know how much we appreciate your work, your leadership, your sense of humanity and compassion. You're a real asset to the department.

ADAM: Thank you.

BEATRIX: Everyone loves you, Dr. Bright. Your kindness and common sense are the best among the many people who have been in your position. We're so glad you came and we're so glad you're staying through these troubled times.

ADAM: (*Sighs*) Yes, I appreciate your kind words and your faith in my abilities.

BEATRIX: Faith? We are all true believers in you. It's astonishing how you've captured the hearts and minds of everyone in the department, from the upper administration to the janitors. (*Approaches ADAM but remains at a six-foot distance and with her mask*). If we weren't in these times, I'd give you a hug.

ADAM: (*Holds up his hand*) No, please. I believe you. (*Pauses*) I've grown very fond of everyone here. And I'm continually impressed by your dedication, experience and talent. (*Pauses*) But the wear and tear of this job on my family has become intolerable.

BEATRIX: What are you saying?

ADAM: I need to resign and move on.

BEATRIX: (*Returns to her desk and sits down*) How can we avoid this? Do you need some time off? Another assistant? An increase in salary?

ADAM: Those are all kind offers, but I can tell that it's just not possible to satisfy the needs of this position and establish a meaningful work-life balance.

BEATRIX: We're all confronted with that same conflict. There are ways to resolve it.

ADAM: No, it isn't possible given my roles and responsibilities. At some point, I just have to place my family and my health first.

BEATRIX: Take a week off. Think about this.

ADAM: The last time I took time off, I spent hours on my phone dealing with problems. There is just no one who can take on the same tasks at the same level.

BEATRIX: Of course, we can! They can send personnel issues through me and send the hiring and medical issues through one of your colleagues.

ADAM: They're all busy enough already. It's not possible to add additional burdens on them.

BEATRIX: And if you leave? What situation will that leave us in? Will that be any better than a temporary vacation?

ADAM: Government is made to grind forward and we're all just cogs in the big wheel. One missing cog does not stop the whole machinery. None of us is indispensable and failure is only guaranteed if the position has been created that way.

BEATRIX: Why would anyone create a job like that?

ADAM: I don't know. (*Pauses*) It's just that every system is perfectly designed to produce the results it produces.

BEATRIX: That's cynical.

ADAM: No, just realistic.

BEATRIX: Do you feel you were set up for failure?

ADAM: Not exactly, but I threw myself into this heart, body and soul and just could not make it work. I may not be the smartest, hardest working man in the world, but I certainly represent the average man. And if I couldn't make it work, who could? The next guy? The next woman?

BEATRIX: That remains to be seen. (*Pauses*) And when will you leave?

ADAM: At the end of the month.

BEATRIX: This is going to make a lot of people very unhappy.

BY THE LETTER

ADAM: It makes me unhappy, too. You can't just turn your back on friends and colleagues without a feeling of betrayal, especially in the middle of a pandemic.

BEATRIX: Please don't flagellate yourself with guilt. Better to leave at the height of your glory than when you pissed off enough people in the department or the legislature to be asked to move on. Maybe you just have a good sense of timing.

ADAM: Good sense of timing, like all the others before me in this position?

BEATRIX: They didn't all leave in glory, you know.

ADAM: So, I hear.

BEATRIX: As sorry as I am to see you to go, I don't think you could have done anything more. With a little luck, your strategic planning initiative will go on to bear some fruit.

ADAM: Sour grapes, perhaps?

BEATRIX: No, real change.

ADAM: Do you really think people want change? If every system is perfectly designed to produce the results it produces, then maybe real, substantive change isn't what people want.

BEATRIX: Where does that leave me?

ADAM: Right where you are, in a position of power and authority, with a sense of security borne from controlling the situation.

BEATRIX: I don't control the situation any more than you do. In fact, with your brains, your talent and your sparkling personality, you can pick and choose your job anywhere.

ADAM: But I wanted to be here where people need change and I was willing to propose it.

BEATRIX: Who can move a bureaucracy? Who can redirect the Titanic in time, even if you see the iceberg ahead.

ADAM: Maybe I just want to jump ship before it strikes.

BEATRIX: Don't worry. A lot of us have life boats already prepared.

ADAM: So, I hear.

BEATRIX: (*Pauses*) We just have to survive the next administration and the next and the next. While you fortunate few in the upper administration change with the political seasons, we trudge on, year after year, governor after governor, fixed and immovable, hunkered down against the vagaries of the political prevailing winds.

ADAM: Very nautical, if somewhat depressing.

BEATRIX: Survival is always depressing. Some live, some die. Some stay, some go. Some retire and others get fired. It's the wheel of bureaucratic life.

ADAM: And I need to get rolling along, too. The Buddhist wheel of life has concentric upward spirals, so it spins and ascends at the same time. That's the wheel I want to be on.

BEATRIX: Best of luck and don't be surprised if you get a prolonged, tearful farewell.

ADAM: With a celebratory mass?

BEATRIX: No, this is the secular state after all. But I wouldn't count out some holy candles and incense. Best of luck.

BY THE LETTER

ADAM: Thanks for your constant support and advice. It was greatly appreciated.

BEATRIX: My pleasure. Greetings to your wife and family. (*Bows and sits down as she shakes her head slowly*) There goes another one.

SCENE III

This time, it is ADAM at the desk and ANTHONY enters without knocking (or wearing a mask) and strides up to the desk. ADAM stands to greet him.

ADAM: Senator LaFleur, so nice to see you again (*sticks out his elbow to ANTHONY.*)

ANTHONY: (*Does not reciprocate and pulls up a chair to sit down*) Nice seeing you, too, Doctor Bright.

ADAM: Call me Adam, please.

ANTHONY: Okay, Adam. You can call me Senator LaFleur, please.

ADAM: Of course, Senator, whatever you like. (*Pauses*) To what do I owe the pleasure?

ANTHONY: Well, not sure it's a pleasure, but I wanted to discuss your recent appearances before the legislature.

ADAM: Of course, Senator. What about them?

ANTHONY: You've been giving alarming statistics about death and disease progression in this pandemic which my constituents claim are inflated and even fabricated.

BY THE LETTER

ADAM: Inflated and fabricated?

ANTHONY: Yes, precisely. They believe you're making up numbers to create a climate of fear and prevent the economy from opening up.

ADAM: Mr. Senator, we have some of the most accurate statistics in the country. If anything, cases are under-reported because people will not answer the phone for the contract tracers. And, if they do, they claim they have never been out of quarantine.

ANTHONY: Maybe they haven't and maybe they're telling the truth and you just don't want to believe them.

ADAM: Forty percent don't answer and 50% of those say they never interacted with a living soul in the preceding two weeks. How can we contract trace effectively like that? How can we stop the transmission of this virus?

ANTHONY: Don't stop it! Let people get sick so we get herd immunity. I'm sure you know what that is.

ADAM: Of course, and it won't work until you have 70% of people infected.

ANTHONY: And how many do we have infected?

ADAM: Maybe ten percent. (*Pauses*) You'd have to let the disease spread to another 60% of the population. That would double or triple the death toll among the most vulnerable people in the population, the old, the sick, the poor, the Blacks and Hispanics.

ANTHONY: There has been so many untruths from your department that no one knows what to believe.

ADAM: Minor discrepancies are unavoidable.

ANTHONY: HA! Ten percent is minor? I'd love to hear what a major discrepancy is.

ADAM: The state auditor declared the statistics reliable. Your own state auditor.

ANTHONY: Perhaps we ought to change the subject. I did hear that our children had a minor altercation at school.

ADAM: That was your son?

ANTHONY: Yes, and he used some inappropriate language at school. That much I'll concede. (*Pauses*) But he was provoked.

ADAM: Provoked?

ANTHONY: He overheard you son saying that it was okay for kids to have two moms or two dads and that they might sleep in the same bed like you and your wife.

ADAM: Precocious, but not inaccurate.

ANTHONY: Children that age are very impressionable. Our son came home traumatized. He had never heard anything like that before. Same sex couples just don't come up at our home. We have Christian values. I said something about people thinking like that were pussies and he must have taken it back to school.

ADAM: He did and my son got the brunt of it. He's not used to being insulted and bullied at school.

ANTHONY: Just some schoolyard banter, that's all. It may have been the first time, but it won't be the last. The world is a cruel place.

ADAM: We teach our son that it is immoral to denigrate other people.

BY THE LETTER

ANTHONY: Well, he certainly won't have a life in politics and you may not either.

ADAM: What's that supposed to mean?

ANTHONY: It means that I heard from reliable sources that you may be resigning. I just wanted to tell you that I think it's a good idea. You don't reflect the values of the people here.

ADAM: There are fine people here, with good educations and decent values. Besides, I'm here to serve the people to the best of my ability, not necessarily reflect their values.

ANTHONY: That may be somewhat true of you, but it certainly isn't true of me. I'm elected to represent the values of those who elected me and they are tired of your outsider values and mis-information. They want straight talk and simple ideas.

ADAM: The truth is always straight and simple.

ANTHONY: Don't lecture me, young man! We'll do the nice thing and let you resign rather than be fired. That way you can have a glorious departure and ride away into the sunset. You'll get glowing reviews and a wonderful letter of recommendation for your future job in a state more compatible with your liberal ideals. (*Pauses*) Why did you come here anyway?

ADAM: I wanted to come to a place that needed good people with new ideas.

ANTHONY: Yes, but to the poorest, sickest, least educated place in the country?

ADAM: Mother Theresa didn't go to Manhattan, she went to the slums of Calcutta.

ANTHONY: Yeah, and every Damien has his Molokai, I know. I've heard you quoted already.

ADAM: Precisely.

ANTHONY: I need to be getting along. I think we've reached an understanding here. Goodbye and good luck (*turns and strides out the door.*)

SCENE IV

ADAM and CHRISTINA are packing boxes in their home. ADAM holds up an alligator head.

ADAM: Remember this?

CHRISTINA: Yes, you had to hide it away at night so the kids wouldn't have nightmares.

ADAM: It's a bit creepy.

CHRISTINA: *(Holds up a voodoo doll)* And this?

ADAM: Yes, that's pretty creepy, too. A gift from my devoted chief of staff and others. (*Turns it over and reads*) "To Dr. Adam Bright from his devoted staff." Nice.

CHRISTINA: (Hold*s up a plate with a magnolia blossom*) This is beautiful, too. Can't say I'm a big fan of magnolia blossoms. But it's well done. Almost big enough for a turkey platter.

ADAM: (*Picks up a paperweight and holds it to the light*) Looks like a seascape with some sea anemones. It will be nice getting back to the coast, don't you think?

CHRISTINA: Yes.

ADAM: Did you like anything about this place?

CHRISTINA: Of course! There were some very fine people here, just not enough of them. It also seemed like there was a miasma in the air, something half-decayed, the weight of history.

ADAM: The burden of Southern history.

CHRISTINA: Yes, exactly.

ADAM: I did meet some extraordinary people here, some saints and some sinners. *(Pauses)* But you're right. There was a heaviness about it, something ancient and sinister, something about slavery.

CHRISTINA: You know what Faulkner wrote, don't you?

ADAM: He wrote many things.

CHRISTINA: "The past in not dead, it's not even past."

ADAM stands up and approaches CHRISTINA and gives her a hug.

ADAM: Thanks for sticking with me. I'm not always that easy to live with.

CHRISTINA: No one is. (*Looks around*) Let's finish packing. It's time to leave.

BLACK OUT

THAT'S LIFE

THAT'S LIFE

CHARACTERS

    THEODORA: Young Black woman.

    CLARISE: Pro-life activist.

    CHAQUETTA: Public health worker.

SETTING

    Non-descript office setting with three chairs and a table.

THEODORA: I can't afford this baby. I didn't really want it. I just missed a few pills by accident and there you go (*points to her belly*).

CLARISE: We can help.

THEODORA: Get an abortion?

CLARISE: We don't encourage that, but if you decide to go that way, we can't prevent you. We just provide alternative strategies. (*Pauses*) How many weeks are you?

THEODORA: I'm not sure.

CLARISE: No idea at all?

THEODORA: My last period was 8 weeks ago and the health unit nurse said I was pregnant and gave me some pre-natal vitamins and got me signed up for Medicaid.

CLARISE: Who do you have at home to help you?

THEODORA: My grandma, that's all.

CLARISE: Are you employed?

THEODORA: Yeah, I'm a CNA at the nursing home. (*Pauses*) Bad job, low pay, no insurance (*pauses*) I can't take care of a baby now, I just don't have the time or money.

CLARISE: We'll get you an ultrasound and a blood test to figure out how far you're along.

THEODORA: (*Stands up*) I don't want an ultrasound to see this baby or hear the heartbeat. That's what you do to girls who come here. I don't want to get attached if it's going to be gone in a few days.

CLARISE: It's part of our procedure to better serve you. Once we get through the first exam, it's a lot easier.

THEODORA: I'm calling my nurse friend. Can she join us?

CLARISE: Of course, everyone's welcome.

THEODORA: (*Calls on her cell phone*) Hello, Chaquetta, I'm over her at the Family Life place. You know, the one on Lee Street. (*Pauses*) Yes, I know I'm pregnant. (*Pauses*) Can you join me here. You said I could call you anytime. (*Pauses*) Good. I'll see you in a few minutes.

BY THE LETTER

CLARISE: (*Shows some papers*) We offer free counselling, free diapers, WIC referrals, home visiting and lot's more, even toys and a crib. Everything you might need.

THEODORA: Can I get an abortion pill prescription?

CLARISE: No, that's against our principles. Besides, it's probably too late for that now. It only works in the first few days of conception.

THEODORA: I'm worried about that, too. I should have taken that Plan B pill after we had sex, but I didn't think I'd missed enough birth control pills to get pregnant. (*Pauses*) I just can't handle a baby now. It's just me. No husband. Not even a steady boyfriend.

CLARISE: There's always adoption. That's another option for you. We can make those referrals and there's lots of nice families out there who would love a new baby.

THEODORA: No! No flesh and blood of mine's going to some strangers, even if they want a baby.

CLARISE: These are good people, well-to-do people who are desperate for a child because they can't have one of their own. Your baby could have They don't care about the sex or the race.

THEODORA: (*Swings around*) No baby of mine is going to a stranger to raise like they want. It's unnatural.

>*CHAQUETTA enters the room and turns toward CLARISE.*

CHAQUETTA: (*To CLARISE*) Hello, I'm Chaquetta Wilson. (*To THEODORA*) Hello, Theodora. Nice to see you again.

THEODORA: You told me I could get pregnant and if I missed two pills and here I am, maybe eight weeks.

CLARISE: (*To CHAQUETTA*) You got here awfully fast. Were you waiting outside?

CHAQUETTA: No, I just happened to be off work and went to Home Depot down the road. It's less than five minutes away. No big deal. (*To THEODORA*) How can I help you.

THEODORA: I can't have this baby. I can barely get by now. (*Pauses*) How could I support a baby?

CLARISE: We can help.

THEODORA: If you can, then give me a referral to an abortion clinic and let's be done with this.

CLARISE: (*To CHAQUETTA*) Do you support that? The murder of unborn child?

CHAQUETTA: We support what is best for the patient. (*Pauses*) In the first place, we try and avoid unintended pregnancy, but that's a tough thing to do.

THEODORA: Tell me about it! Two days of missed pills and wham! I'm pregnant.

CLARISE: What about the child's best interest? What about God's will? I thought Theodora meant a lover of God.

THEODORA: That's Greek to me. (*Pauses*) I have my own way of loving God.

CLARISE: By killing unborn babies.

CHAQUETTA: (*To CLARISE*) That's enough of that kind of language. Besides, as an organization, we don't have any religious affiliation or any religious agenda.

BY THE LETTER

CLARISE: That's obvious.

CHAQUETTA: I hold religious beliefs personally, but our organization doesn't. It's secular.

CLARISE: So, secular beliefs like those of your organization support and facilitate the murder of unborn babies. That's okay with you?

CHAQUETTA: Ma'am, I'm not here to here to discuss philosophy, but to help Theodora out in a difficult decision.

CLARISE: By murdering her baby?

CHAQUETTA: No, by letting her make up her own mind. We don't murder babies.

THEODORA: No one's talking about murdering babies. This (*points to her belly and puts her hand there*) is a fetus, not a baby. In my family, still in the belly means the baby can't survive, at least not this early.

CLARISE: That fetus has arms, legs, a brain, a soul.

CHAQUETTA: A soul?

CLARISE: Yes, a soul.

CHAQUETTA: Since when? Four months? 2 months, one month?

CLARISE: At conception.

THEODORA: Conception?

CLARISE: As soon as the egg is fertilized by the sperm, life begins and the soul takes flight.

THEODORA: Sounds like a bird.

CLARISE: No, like an angel, God's angel. Life seeking life. Love seeking love, the culmination of God's will.

THEODORA: Yeah, but God doesn't pay my rent or buy my groceries or pay for my doctor's bills. (*Pauses*) I wish he did, and my utilities, too.

CLARISE: Seek first the Kingdom of Heaven and all things will be given unto you.

CHAQUETTA: Can we get back to the business at hand?

CLARISE: She's not business, she's a human being with another human being inside of her who both have temporary problems. Let's approach her on a human level, not a business one.

THEODORA: I'm human.

CLARISE: Exactly.

CHAQUETTA: (*To THEODORA*) Do you want to have this baby or not?

THEODORA: (*Pauses*) I'm not really sure anymore. If this lady is going to buy my groceries, pay my rent and utilities and take care of the baby, maybe it's okay to go ahead and have it.

CLARISE: (*Hesitates*) That's not exactly what we can do for you.

THEODORA: You just said God was going to take care of it. (*To CHAQUETTA*) Didn't she?

CHAQUETTA: More or less.

CLARISE: We can help you have the baby and get you some assistance and even arrange an adoption, but we can't buy your groceries or pay your rent.

BY THE LETTER

THEODORA: "Some" assistance is not enough.

CLARISE: The world has unlimited demands and there are only limited resources. We have to deal with that fact daily. Everyone can't have everything they want.

CHAQUETTA: (*To THEODORA*) If you want me to help you out, come to my office tomorrow.

CLARISE: Or you can start with us today.

THEODORA: Fighting over me like two street dogs. I kind of like the attention. (*Puts her hand on her belly*) So does the baby.

CLARISE: Does it have a name yet?

THEODORA: Fetus.

CLARISE: Fetus?

THEODORA: That's the name now. (*Pauses*) And fetus and I need to get going. I got a shift at 2 pm at the nursing home and if I'm late, they fire you.

CHAQUETTA: (*Hands THEODORA her card*) Here's my card again. You know where the office is located. And that's the office number and that's my cell number. I think you have them both on your cell phone. Call any time.

CLARISE: And here's my card. My cell number's on the back.

THEODORA: So much attention. It almost makes me feel wanted. Maybe that's what being pregnant is all about, being wanted or at least having the impression you're wanted. (*Pauses*) No one cares a hoot about you until you have this precious cargo, planned or not. After the baby's born, no one give a damn whether you or the baby live or die.

CHAQUETTA: I care about you, pregnant or not. Finish your GED, get a nursing degree and have a better life than the one you're living. If you think being pregnant and having a baby will help you improve your life, then go for it. If you don't, then we're here to help you.

CLARISE: (*To CHAQUETTA*) I hope you and your organization lose all of your funding and shut down. No one needs your murder mill.

CHAQUETTA: And I wish you the best, too. I think it's time for Theodora and I to leave. (*To THEODORA*) Need a ride?

THEODORA: That would be great, Auntie. (*To CLARISE*). You couldn't ask for a better aunt than Chaquetta. She's been helping me and my family forever. I'm really lucky to have her in the family.

> *THEODORA and CHAQUETTA begin to exit.*

CLARISE: (*Calls after them*) At least take this plastic 8-week fetus to remind you of what you want to destroy.

THEODORA: (*Turns and looks at the fetus*) No thanks, that's too creepy.

> *THEODORA and CHAQUETTA exit. CLARISE sinks back into her chair in an attitude of despair.*

BLACKOUT

GOING TO ZAGREB

CHARACTERS

>NATALIE: Older woman, foreign accent. Mother of THEODORE.

>THEODORE: Mid-thirties. Tall, slender, articulate. Speaks with some affectation.

>HEATHER: Older woman. Grey-haired spinster. Sister-in-law to NATALIE.

>AURELIE: Young mother in her early 30's. Daughter-in-law to NATALIE.

SETTING

>Room with a large map of Eastern Europe which is used as a reference during the discussion. It must show Croatia, Greece and Turkey.

AURELIE: I can't go on this trip!

NATALIE: Why?

AURELIE: What if I get COVID and I get stuck in Istanbul (*points to Istanbul on the map*) and can't get home on time? I might miss Christmas with my children.

NATALIE: We're all vaccinated and have gotten boosters. You're not likely to get COVID if we're careful.

AURELIE: Likely? That's not enough for me. I want to be certain and it's just not the time to be wandering around Eastern Europe.

HEATHER: Will it ever be the time? Besides, there's no such thing as absolute certainty.

AURELIE: Yes, of course there will be a time. This pandemic won't last forever and someday it will be safer.

HEATHER: (*To THEODORE*) You live in Europe, is it that dangerous?

NATALIE: The State Department says all those countries are "4."

THEODORE: That means do NOT travel there at this time.

AURELIE: If the State Department says that, then I'm with them. . .don't go.

HEATHER: Such patriotic zeal.

THEODORE: I do live over there (*points to a place in France*). I'm not dead yet and I'm vaccinated and I never got COVID.

NATALIE: (*To AURELIE*) But if you don't go, it will just be the four of us.

HEATHER: Maybe not.

NATALIE: What does that mean?

BY THE LETTER

HEATHER: I'm having problems with the airlines. They've already cancelled my flight twice. I'm already going to arrive late and I might get stuck going out.

NATALIE: You can always catch up with us later on the trip in Split or Athens (*points to those two cities on the map*). Or even Istanbul for that matter.

THEODORE: That's part of the problem. Three countries in a time of COVID. What a hassle! They're testing coming into a country, testing leaving it, testing going to the next place and a bunch of paperwork. There's a "person locator" in Greece and a "health certificate" in Turkey and maybe even an eVisa there, too. It's just not worth it.

AURELIE: My point, exactly. It's not worth it.

NATALIE: This is supposed to be a fun family trip. Dad's got his heart set on it. He's been dreaming about it for 20 months, learning Croatian, Greek and Turkish.

THEODORE: Let him go alone.

NATALIE: Fat chance! He won't even go to a movie alone, much less to Zagreb (*points to Zagreb on the map.*)

AURELIE: Or Athens (*points to Athens*).

THEODORE: Or Istanbul (*points to Istanbul*).

NATALIE: Don't bail out on me, please! If Aurelie doesn't go, or Heather, that just leaves you (*points to THEODORE*). You're my last chance.

THEODORE: Seventeen days with Dad! I love to travel, but even a week with him is overwhelming.

AURELIE: He can be intense.

HEATHER: Intense? Is that the word?

NATALIE: How about fanatically. (*To AURELIE*) I understand you're worrying about your kids, but you can experience Croatia, Greece and Turkey. You would never do that with your parents.

AURELIE: They are a bit set in their ways.

NATALIE: And they're filling your head with visions of terrorists, abductions, rapes and murder.

THEODORE: (*Laughs*) Really? That's ridiculous. People travel there all the time and its perfectly safe, especially for tourists.

AURELIE: That's not what I hear. Bombings, ISIS, kidnappings with ransoms.

HEATHER: That's Syria, not Turkey.

AURELIE: Doesn't Turkey border Syria?

THEODORE: Yeah, hundreds of miles from where we will be going (*points to Syria on the map*).

AURELIE: My geography's not that good.

HEATHER: So, you're definitely out?

AURELIE: (*Sheepishly*) Yes, I'm out. I would worry about my babies the whole time. It wouldn't be fun at all. I would just imagine getting stuck in Istanbul and isolated for 14 days all alone. No Christmas. No tree. No gifts. No children. (*Pauses*) No! I'm definitely out.

NATALIE: And you, HEATHER?

HEATHER: I'm waffling, but the negatives keep growing and the positives keep shrinking.

THEODORE: The flights?

HEATHER: Not just that. It's all those forms to fill out from country to country and maybe a couple of hundred bucks for a Turkish eVisa. It's all a bit crazy.

NATALIE: It can't be the money. You're rich!

HEATHER: I'm rich because I live frugally.

THEODORE: Nothing wrong with that!

NATALIE: (*To THEODORE*) Yes, we know. You've lived on bananas and rice for years. No wonder you are so skinny.

HEATHER: And you smoke.

NATALIE: Yes, it's all very European.

THEODORE: Nothing wrong with that. Besides, I could never be happy living in the United States.

NATALIE: Then you should be overjoyed with an all-expenses paid trip, free meals, free hotels, and free guided tours to Eastern Europe.

AURELIE: What's not to like?

THEODORE: (*To AURELIE*) You're not even coming, so maybe you should refrain from commenting.

NATALIE: (*To THEODORE*) Looks like I can't even pay you to come along. (*Pauses*) Think of all the fun we'll have.

HEATHER: I'm not going either. The flight uncertainty, the forms, the COVID testing and in three countries no less. No, I'm not going either.

NATALIE: And traveling with Dad. It that it? (*To THEODORE*) Is that the real issue?

THEODORE: He gets on my nerves, no doubt about that. He runs from museum to museum, from theatre to theatre, from concert to concert. It's never a vacation, it's always a race against the clock.

NATALIE: Tell me about it. We've been married 40 years.

AURELIE and HEATHER: Forty!

NATALIE: Forty years of catering to his whims, fixing his meals, following him to every cultural venue, doing his laundry and receiving a parade of guests from everywhere in the world.

HEATHER: We're talking about 17 days here, not 40 years.

NATALIE: (*To HEATHER*) But you're not going either, so please don't comment. (*To THEODORE*) That only leaves you.

AURELIE: And Dad.

NATALIE: (*To THEODORE*) So it's up to you.

THEODORE: Don't put this on my shoulders.

NATALIE: If you don't go, I'm cancelling the trip.

AURELIE and HEATHER: Really?

NATALIE: YES!

THEODORE: You're really piling the pressure on me.

BY THE LETTER

NATALIE: A 17 day paid vacation, single room (*points to the map*) four days in Croatia, (*moves her finger*) 5 days in Greece and (*points her finger*) 5 in Turkey.

THEODORE: Sounds exhausting. And that's not even factoring in Dad.

NATALIE: Tell me about it.

AURELIE: Dad's got his heart set on this trip. These are all places he loves. Art, history, music, folk dancing. (*To NATALIE*) He's been working really hard for 20 months and he's been talking about this trip forever.

HEATHER: He hasn't had any vacations, but lots of stress working at the shelter, the vaccinations, the testing, the deployments, working at the office and home. He's really wants this trip. He needs this trip.

NATALIE: (*To HEATHER*) You're out of this, too. Please refrain from comments.

HEATHER: I just know him. (*Pauses*) You cancel the trip and he'll blow his stack. He'll never forgive you.

NATALIE: You're not helping. If you're not joining us, then I don't need any guilt trips or fear-mongering.

THEODORE: God, I'm glad I'll be thousands of miles away if you cancel the trip.

NATALIE: He's been studying Croatian, Greek and Turkish every night for months.

HEATHER: You've got to be kidding.

NATALIE: No, I'm not. He bought three small books that stay on his bedside table. Every night he does a few pages, memorizing common words and phrases.

AURELIE: What discipline.

NATALIE: (*To AURELIE*) Remember, you're out of this!

HEATHER: What fanaticism! (*To AURELIE*) I wouldn't be worried about getting abducted by ISIS. Your father-in-law's already fanatic enough.

NATALIE: And I'm married to him. Trapped in happiness. (*To THEODORE*) So what's it going to be? Going or not?

THEODORE: I can't do it!

NATALIE: (*Grabs THEODORE*) Don't leave me along with him for 17 days.

AURELIE: You've been married 40 years. What's a few more days?

NATALIE: It's not the same. At home, I can go into the den and read or watch "Criminal Minds" while he's typing away at some stupid stories or plays that no one will ever read. At home, we're together, but with space. He goes to work and I have a whole day of "me time."

THEODORE: I can relate.

HEATHER: Not being married, I'm not sure I can.

AURELIE: And I'm still very much in love at this point. So, that's hard for me to imagine.

NATALIE: It's true. (*Pauses*) Being at home is like being on a cruise ship. We can always go our separate ways and come back together for meals.

THEODORE: But being trapped together in airports, on planes, in vans, in museums, in hotels an in restaurants. And Dad spouting off his twenty words of Croatian, Greek or Turkish.

BY THE LETTER

HEATHER: Or Spanish.

AURELIE: Or French.

THEODORE: It's annoying as hell.

NATALIE: Yes, it is! And both of us crammed together for 17 straight days. (*Pauses*) I can't take it alone. I just can't.

THEODORE: You're going to have to somehow.

NATALIE: NO! If you're all out, I'm out too.

HEATHER: So, you're cancelling.

NATALIE: (*Almost in tears*) I have to.

HEATHER: Do you think he'll go alone?

NATALIE: I doubt it.

HEATHER: Didn't he cancel something else just to make sure he could go on this trip?

NATALIE: Yes, he cancelled his stupid play-soldier trip.

THEODORE: (*To HEATHER*) DMAT.

NATALIE: Yes, Disaster Medical Assistance Team. Adults in uniform. Boy scouts for do-gooders. Deployments to God knows where.

AURELIE: What happened?

NATALIE: He stupidly signed up for this month, knowing full well it almost ran right into our European trip. I warned him I'd cancel our European trip if he went off on deployment.

THEODORE: Well, now it looks like he won't be doing either. All his time and yours are freed up for something else.

NATALIE: For what?

HEATHER: More "me time" for you.

NATALIE: He'll be sulking around, sullen and resentful for days, weeks, months.

HEATHER: Shouldn't he be?

NATALIE: (*To HEATHER*) You're not helping. (*Pauses*) I want family time, not couple time.

THEODORE: Not "me time?"

NATALIE: (*Pauses*) Maybe a little.

HEATHER: So, when are you going to pull the plug?

NATALIE: I'm doing it tonight after he gets back from work.

THEODORE: A great way to end a busy day.

NATALIE: All his days are busy.

HEATHER: And his nights, too, from the sounds of it. Always working on something.

NATALIE: Yes, he's always doing something. He's living drama, always drama. Conflicts with colleagues, bosses, subordinates. Always a righteous battle somewhere with someone.

THEODORE: And don't forget the stage. He's writing it when he's not living it. A regular Don Quixote.

NATALIE: Don't remind me. His plays get rejected, his art gets rejected, his teaching role got cancelled...

HEATHER: And now, this!

THEODORE: Rejected by his wife of 40 years, too. That's a lot. I can relate, it's got to be tough.

AURELIE: (*To THEODORE*) And we're all adding to the rejection now.

THEODORE: A quadruple whammy!

HEATHER: (*To NATALIE*) Don't worry. He'll survive. He'll write some stupid play that no one will read and no one will perform.

AURELIE: All this rejection and he was just elected Man-of-the-Year by the local paper, right? That contradiction has got to hurt.

NATALIE: Man-of-the-Year, indeed! His thirst for adulation is unquenchable. Trust me, I've watched him up close for 40 years.

THEODORE: Watch out. He'll end up a bitter old man.

AURELIE: Alone.

NATALIE: Who knows? Maybe?

HEATHER: He's already isolated. No soul brothers in this little town.

NATALIE: That's true.

AURELIE: And just one soul sister?

NATALIE: (*Looks startled*) Who?

AURELIE: You, of course.

NATALIE: (*Sighs*) I used to think so, but I'm not so sure anymore. Maybe that's why I don't want to go on this trip. I don't want to look across the table and think that I'm spending time with a man I don't love anymore.

THEODORE: Pretty heavy, Mom. And all this over a trip to Zagreb?

HEATHER: And Athens (*points to the map*).

AURELIE: And Istanbul (*points to the map*).

NATALIE: (*Looks around*) You've all pushed me into a corner.

AURELIE: That's not fair.

NATALIE: It's true! I can take it from a sister-in-law (*points to HEATHER*) and a daughter-in-law (*points to AURELIE*). (*Points to THEODORE*) But from my own flesh and blood? That's tough.

THEODORE: I have my own sanity to worry about. It's fragile.

NATALIE: We'll be dead and gone and you'll all be still thinking about this calamity, this aborted trip to Croatia (*points to the map*) and Greece (*points to the map*).

HEATHER: And Turkey (*points to the map*).

NATALIE: And how you precipitated a crisis and stood back and watched the disaster unfold.

THEODORE: Talk about a guilt trip. (*Pauses*) My answer is still no.

NATALIE: (*To AURELIE*) And you?

AURELIE: No.

NATALIE: (*To HEATHER*) And you?

BY THE LETTER

HEATHER: No!

NATALIE: Then it's a done deal. I've made my decision. I'll accept the consequences.

AURELIE: Dad will forgive you.

NATALIE: Will he? I think not. This trip was way too important for him. He's too invested financially and emotionally. Maybe this whole project wasn't ever a trip at all, but the end of the road for both of us.

AURELIE: We can always go to Disneyworld next year?

NATALIE: Fat chance.

HEATHER: Or someplace else as a family when COVID's finally gone.

THEODORE: COVID will never be gone.

NATALIE: No, it won't. He can't even get people vaccinated here and the world's full of unvaccinated people.

AURELIE: See! I'm right to worry about getting COVID.

HEATHER: Appropriate worry and unjustified anxieties are not the same thing.

THEODORE: So, where do we go from here?

NATALIE: I don't know, but it won't be Zagreb, Athens or Istanbul.

HEATHER: It's going to break his heart.

THEODORE: "The world breaks everyone, but some people get stronger in the broken places." Hemingway wrote that.

NATALIE: Well, let's hope it's true here, too, and he's one of the ones who heals. (*Goes and gets a bottle of wine*) I think we need this. (*Pours four glasses and passes them out. Raises her glass*) To Zagreb!

ALL: (*Raise their glasses*) To Zagreb!

BLACKOUT

NOT TAKING THE SHOT

CHARACTERS

    GLADYS: 50-year-old female (any race), modest means, simple clothing.

    BARNABY: 50-year-old male (any race), modest means, simple clothing.

    REVERAND HARPER: Distinguished man in his mid-sixties. Dressed in dark clothing.

SETTING

    Interior of a modest home.

TIME

    Winter 2020

BARNABY: I'm not taking that COVID shot. I don't care who's giving it or if it's free or not.

GLADYS: You're a fool! You want to get COVID and die?

BARNABY: Die? That damn thing hasn't killed a person I know, not one.

GLADYS: What about that chicken guy?

BARNABY: Cain?

GLADYS: Yes, that one. He went to some fool political rally and caught COVID and died.

BARNABY: Maybe, but the President got it already and he looked better after he was sick than before.

GLADYS: Yeah, pumped full of steroids and experimental medicine by the finest doctors at Walter Reed Hospital. (*Pauses*) Well, if you won't take the shot, what about me?

BARNABY: You're as healthy as a horse. You wouldn't die, even if you got it.

GLADYS: Maybe I look healthy, but I'm not.

BARNABY: What do you mean?

GLADYS: The doctor told me I have high sugar and it has already affecting my kidneys and my eyes.

BARNABY: You seem to pee pretty regular to me, even a few times at night. How come you didn't tell me before?

GLADYS: I didn't want to bother you. (*Pauses*) Something in my blood told him my kidneys were only working about a third of normal.

BARNABY: I don't believe it.

GLADYS: Don't believe it, you old fool, but that doesn't change a thing. (*Pauses*) Plus I already lost a quarter of my eyesight.

BARNABY: You see just fine. You read those credit card bills and tell me what I spent before I get back into the house. Don't tell me you can't see.

GLADYS: (*Pulls out a magnifying glass*) This is how I do it.

BARNABY: Since when?

GLADYS: For the last seven months.

BARNABY: You didn't think that was worth telling me either? (*Pauses*) So, what does all of this have to do with COVID?

GLADYS: If I get COVID, I'm high risk and can die. (*Pauses*) Do you want me to die?

BARNABY: Of course not! (*Pauses*) But you can just as easily get COVID from that nursing home where you work.

GLADYS: Lots of COVID there. (*Pauses*) But now they check the old people every week and about a third of them have already had it.

BARNABY: See! It's all of those old folks that are the problem. Let'em get COVID and die.

GLADYS: It's the staff members that brought it in and got the poor residents infected. We had three ladies from the kitchen who all got it. And the whole food service got shut down. (*Pauses*) We had to step in and help cook and serve and feed the residents for a couple of weeks. You better believe those old folks will be getting the vaccine as soon as possible.

BARNABY: Why didn't you tell me about this?

GLADYS: You didn't seem interested.

BARNABY: That's crazy! Of course, I'm interested, especially if you're going to get the COVID and bring it back to me. (*Pauses*) Why don't you quit that job and get something else that's less dangerous?

GLADYS: What job? Lots of jobs have gone away since the COVID and my skills aren't that great. Besides, I'm pretty old.

BARNABY: Fifty-five isn't that old. (*Pauses*) I didn't tell you, but old Mrs. LaCroix down on Military Highway just died.

GLADYS: COVID?

BARNABY: That's what they say.

GLADYS: Why didn't you tell me? You said you didn't know anyone who died. That's a bald-faced lie.

BARNABY: I didn't want you to get upset. You've got enough things on your mind.

GLADYS: Poor lady! Sick and lonely, but with a heart of gold. She gave her kids and grandkids all her money and she lived in misery. (*Pauses*) Good thing she's going to heaven.

BARNABY: Yeah, but I'm not sure she was such a lady.

GLADYS: Why would you say such a thing?

BARNABY: I heard her son was born before she was married.

GLADYS: So?

BARNABY: So, she had a child out of wedlock.

BY THE LETTER

GLADYS: That she raised on her own and treated like a little prince after her second husband left her. Yes, I'm sure she was a lady. And are you such a gentleman?

BARNABY: My soul is at peace.

GLADYS: And would it still be at peace if you killed me through your ignorance and selfishness? Would you still be at peace if I die and you can't even hold my hand in the hospital or have a decent funeral service? (*Pauses*) Would you still be at peace then?

> *Knock at the door. GLADYS goes and opens the door and REVEREND HARPER enters. BARNABY rises and extends his hand. HARPER rejects the hand and extends an elbow. HARPER and BARNABY exchange elbow rubs.*

HARPER: Good evening Sister Gladys, Brother Barnaby. Have you got a minute to spare for an old preacher?

BARNABY and GLADYS: Of course.

GLADYS: How can we help you?

HARPER: (*Sits down and puts his Bible on the coffee table*) I need your assistance.

BARNABY: What exactly do you have in mind? We already tithed this month and money's awful short in this household.

HARPER: We've got some real problems in the congregation. Several people lost their jobs. A bunch of folks are facing eviction. And we have funeral expenses for half a dozen people who can't pay a dime.

GLADYS: (*To BARNABY*) See! I told you folks were dying right and left. (*To HARPER*) I thought you couldn't have funerals.

HARPER: We still have to bury the dead. We just can't hold services with a lot of people.

BARNABY: I guess you do have to bury them. (*Pauses*) Can't you just keep the bodies in those big refrigerator trucks? Looks like those trucks could hold a lot of bodies.

GLADYS: How do you know about such things?

BARNABY: I got eyes (*points to his eyes*) and I see just fine. Besides, I was a logistics specialist in the army. We had to know about such things.

HARPER: No, leaving bodies in a truck is no option. We have seven families with dead loved ones with no place to go. Even cremating them costs money and most of these folks want a real funeral. (*Pauses*) We also got three families who've been evicted and they have no place to live. The mother and children can go into a women's shelter, but the husband would have to go alone to a men's shelter. (*Pauses*) They get one meal a day and can sleep there at night, but they have to go out during the day. They have no place to go but wander around the streets until evening comes. Plus, the shelter won't take anyone who's got COVID and two of the families are infected.

GLADYS: God! You don't want us to take those people into our home, do you?

HARPER: Of course not. That would put you in danger. The only thing we can do is put them up temporarily in a hotel until their isolation or quarantine ends.

GLADYS: And then what?

HARPER: We try and get them back on their feet.

BARNABY: And employment.

HARPER: It's next to impossible. So many places have closed or cut back, there's hardly any jobs left. Except sometimes in hospital and nursing homes. We can also get some jobs as clerks in stores and janitorial staff. (*Pauses*) These people are desperate.

GLADYS: (*Goes to a bureau and pulls out some money*) Here's a hundred dollars.

HARPER: (*Takes the money and nods*) Thank you, Sister Gladys. The Lord loves a cheerful giver.

GLADYS: (*Turns to BARNABY*) And you? You've always got a few bucks stashed away from your retirement check.

HARPER: I don't need any more money. I just need to ask a favor.

BARNABY: What kind of favor?

HARPER: The COVID vaccine is coming out and you are well-respected members of the community. I'd like you both to get vaccinated in public and testify to the safety and usefulness.

GLADYS: Of course.

HARPER: (To BARNABY) And you?

BARNABY: Well. . . .I heard it makes you impotent and sterile.

GLADYS: Impotent? You've been softer than a banana for years. What are you worried about.

BARNABY: A man's got his pride.

HARPER: And pride goes before a fall.

GLADYS: If you won't take it for me, maybe you will take it for God.

BARNABY: Reverend Harper isn't God.

GLADYS: He's God's holy vicar on earth, right? (*Turns to HARPER.*)

HARPER: Let's pray.
> *HARPER, GLADYS and BARNABY all knell down, without joining hands. They raise their arms heavenward.*

HARPER (CONT): Dear Heavenly Father. Bless these, thy servants, Sister Gladys and Brother Barnaby, for agreeing to lead by example by taking the COVID shot and spreading the word about how easy it is to take it. And how it protects them and others around them from serious disease and death. Let them have the courage of their convictions and give courage to others around them in this time of darkness.

GLADYS: Praise the Lord!

HARPER: Let them show the will of God the giver, who showers down his blessing and protects the children of Israel from all pestilence and evil. Who sends us the vaccine to help stop this pestilence.

GLADYS: Give thanks to God!

HARPER: And may you protect them from any harm from disease or infliction as he protected the Israelites from the death he rained down on Pharaoh. Let this vaccine be like the blood on the doors that tells COVID to pass over and spare the children of Israel.

GLADYS: Praise the Lord!

BARNABY: And let his mercy protect those who are unwilling or unable to get the vaccine before it is too late. May God grant them peace! Amen.

GLADYS and BARNABY: Amen.

ALL rise.

GLADYS: (To BARNABY) I'm glad you see the light.

BARNABY: Humph. This was definitely not a social distanced prayer session. (*To HARPER*) I hope you don't have the COVID.

HARPER: I always wear my mask and all prayer sessions are less than 15 minutes and they're greater than 6 feet. (*Pulls out some hand sanitizer and squirts some on his hands and those of GLADYS and BARNABY*). Not exactly communion, but hand sanitizers just might replace Holy Water sometime.

GLADYS and BARNABY: Praise the Lord!

HARPER: And pass the Purell.

GLADYS: And the vaccine.

ALL raise their hands heavenward.

BLACKOUT

THE VIOLIN FESTIVAL

CHARACTERS

    EDUARDO: Violin professor of Hispanic origin. Affable, articulate, clever

    MARIA: Eduardo's wife, also Hispanic, and a talented violinist in her own right.

    CATHERINE: Older woman on the board of the International Violin Festival. Stout, intelligent and no nonsense.

    HENRY: Older man. Catherine's husband. Calm and analytic.

SETTING

    Catherine and Henry's living room. There is a violin case on the coffee table along with some glasses and a bottle of tequila and small shot glasses.

EDUARDO: (*Pours four small glasses of tequila and raises his glass*) *Salud!* To another successful International Violin Competition!

                      Everyone raises their glasses and drinks. EDUARDO fills the glasses again.

BY THE LETTER

CATHERINE: Yes, it was successful. The contestants were happy, the judges were happy and the public almost ignored us. But at least we nearly broke even.

MARIA: I don't think people around here really appreciate the quality of the event and the talents of the contestants. They were all extraordinary, especially the Chinese and Koreans.

EDUARDO: Don't forget the Russians. They were pretty damn good, too. They just didn't win.

HENRY: The event is a world class event, it's just in the wrong place.

EDUARDO: Why do you say that? We were able to stay in the black, attract young people from all over the world and stage an event that many larger cities would envy.

CATHERINE: That's the point, Eduardo, we're not a large city. Look at us. Henry and I and a handful of other local people organize this whole event.

HENRY: And it's subsidized by a tiny group of local donors.

MARIA: Yes, it's a remarkable achievement and you deserve great praise, (*making a wide gesture*) each and every one of you.

EDUARDO: (*Looking at MARIA*) And you and I do, too. We have the musical contacts, we know the judges, we attract the quality of the young musicians by our reputations. Why else would they come to a place like this (*spreading his arms widely*).

CATHERINE: Yes, and you deserve enormous praise as well. Everyone recognizes your artistic talent and your tireless efforts. It's just a lot of work in a very poor, rural, unlikely place.

MARIA: Speaking of artistic contributions and unlikely places. (*To EDUARDO*) Are you going to tell them? Or should I?

EDUARDO: Do you think it's the right time and place?

MARIA: Why not? These are our friends and we are their guests. We've known both of them (*indicates CATHERINE and HENRY*) for years, ever since we came here. They've supported us from the very beginning. Go ahead, tell them.

CATHERINE: (*To MARIA*) You're pregnant!

MARIA: No! (*To EDUARDO*) Go on, tell them.

EDUARDO: I've accepted a job as a professor of violin at Washington University.

HENRY: In St. Louis?

EDUARDO: Yes, in St. Louis. They're looking for someone to build their program and hopefully start an international violin contest of their own.

MARIA: We're so excited. An internationally known university in a big city with a much bigger population. Eduardo will be getting students from all over the world.

EDUARDO: If they give me the right budget, of course.

MARIA: They said they would.

EDUARDO: Trust but verify, Ronald Reagan said that.

HENRY: He did. (*Pauses*) Congratulations to you both! (*Serves more tequilla*) Another toast. To an exciting not beginning in St. Louis. Bravo.

BY THE LETTER

ALL raise their glasses and drink.

MARIA: And I'll be able to join as an associate next year. At least that's what they promised me.

CATHERINE: Congratulations to you both (*embraces both EDUARDO and MARIA*).

Everyone exchanges handshakes or hugs and they all finish their drinks and sit down.

CATHERINE (CONT): I'm so excited for you both. I guess that means the end of the International Violin Festival here.

EDUARDO: Of course not!

HENRY: How will you intend to do that? Being the artistic director for the festival is almost a full-time job.

EDUARDO: This is the 21st Century. We have the internet and Zoom and Skype and all of that. I can continue as artistic director and it will go on just like before.

CATHERINE: That doesn't sound practical.

EDUARDO: What would be the problem?

HENRY: You've been the heart and soul of this festival. If you leave, there's no way we can sustain it. It's your presence in the community that has allowed it to get this far.

EDUARDO: Nonsense. I can fly down here from time to time and otherwise it can all be done at a distance, just like the entries and the recruitment of judges. It's a slice of cake.

MARIA: A piece of cake.

EDUARDO: Thank you.

CATHERINE: I love you both, but there will have to be a local artistic director.

EDUARDO: Who? Why? (*Pauses*) There's no one with my talent, my connections, my organizational skill or may charisma that can pull this off, particularly in this "unlikely" location.

CATHERINE: What about Dr. Chang? He's a fine violinist and has been a soloist with the symphony on several occasions?

EDUARDO: He's a good violinist, a good technician, and I like him, but he's not the caliber that is needed. It would be like replacing a thoroughbred with a draft horse.

HENRY: That's harsh.

EDUARDO: But true.

CATHERINE: And Mr. Shearing, the symphony director? He's well-respected.

EDUARDO: No! He's a fine local conductor, but he plays the oboe, for God's sake, not the violin. What good would that do? Besides, he has no international connections and would wreck everything I've built up over the years.

HENRY: Are you sure?

EDUARDO: I'm positive!

CATHERINE: Henry and I are on the board and everyone likes and respects you, but they're going to want a local artistic director. I can almost guarantee it. That's just the fact of the matter.

BY THE LETTER

MARIA: Are you sure?

CATHERINE: I know these people, I know this town and I know how people think. You leave this town and you will no longer be the artistic director. Perhaps a consultant, but not the artistic director. You know what they say, out of sight, out of mind.

EDUARDO: (*Downs another tequila*) If it's true, I prefer we stop the festival now. This is my baby, my child that I have nurtured with my blood, sweat and tears and I prefer to kill it than to see it fall into the hands of incompetents.

HENRY: That's very extreme.

EDUARDO: No, it's the truth! Let it die. Let it die if I cannot be in total artistic control.

CATHERINE: It's not that simple. We have the community to think about. It's a public activity not a private one.

EDUARDO: That's a lie! It's mine. I conceived it. I sweated blood to make it happen. I catered to rich people who don't know Bach from a banana and now you want me to just quietly go away and give my blessing?

HENRY: Yes, that's it exactly.

EDUARDO: You are both out of your minds!

MARIA: Eduardo! These are our friends.

EDUARDO: Friends don't treat friends like this.

HENRY: (*Pauses*) It sounds like you have the founder's complex.

MARIA: What's that?

HENRY: It's when a company or organization founder feels that they are the owner of the that entity. They feel that no one has the skill or knowledge to carry it forward and would rather see it destroyed than see it pass into other, "incompetent" hands.

CATHERINE: (*Looks at EDUARDO*) Plausible.

EDUARDO: I like you, Henry. I admire you. But don't bore me with some psychological mumbo-jumbo. There's simply no one capable of assuming artistic leadership. It's me or nobody, certainly no one local. Why are you rejecting me when I have done so much for every one of you? You've listened to my playing, my wife's playing and that of hundreds of immensely talented young violinists from all over the world. Every one of them has more talent in their little fingers (*shows his little finger*) than anyone in this whole god-forsaken state.

HENRY: Why did you even bother coming here if it's such a hopeless dump?

EDUARDO: Because everyone has to start somewhere. You have to start at the bottom, maybe even in a dump to be able to claw your way out by work and perseverance.

CATHERINE: You are brilliant. You are talented. You are hard-working. You have brought your talent and organized a wonderful musical event in this little town in this poor, uneducated place. But you can't tele-command a violin festival from St. Louis and expect the same level of fanatical devotion.

MARIA: Fanatical devotion? Is Eduardo a fanatic?

CATHERINE: Just a matter of speech. Nothing political.

MARIA: Eduardo can be a bit overbearing. But his virtues far outweigh his heavy handedness.

BY THE LETTER

EDUARDO: (*To MARIA*) For God's sake, shut up! I don't need to justify anything to these people. We've done everything. We've brought true culture to this wasteland and they cast us out like lepers. It's disgraceful!

HENRY: You're the one who just announced your eminent departure. We're still here (*waves his arms around*), right here in the middle of this cultural desert.

EDUARDO: I'll give you one last opportunity to let me continue as artistic director from my new location in St. Louis. (*Pauses*) You'll never have another opportunity.

CATHERINE: No! We can't do that. I can tell you the board is exhausted. They've given everything they can and that would be just too much. You've given us your time and talent and we've given you our money, our time, and the admiration of the community. There's only so much people around here can offer you. (*Pauses*) Tele-commanding a musical festival from afar will simply not work. We can barely generate the funds now. With you gone, it would be impossible.

EDUARDO: Then it must stop NOW!

MARIA: (*To CATHERINE*) We've been real friends. You helped with my naturalization. You celebrated our children's birthdays. You visited our family in their homes abroad.

EDUARDO: Which I arranged, I might add. No one would have had that sort of experience without me or my connections.

HENRY: Yes, and we're grateful for the experience.

EDUARDO: But what I'm asking is too much. (*Pauses*) I put this hopeless little village on the international map. People came from countries all over the world for a truly world class event. And this should be the end of it. (*Pauses*) So be it! (*To MARIA*) Let's go. Our friends don't want us here anymore and I don't want to stay. Let's continue in a world class city with an international reputation.

CATHERINE and HENRY: St. Louis?

MARIA: Is it that bad?

CATHERINE: Nicer than Cleveland, but it still has its problems.

HENRY: I'm sure you'll be a huge asset to that area.

EDUARDO: Of course, we will.

HENRY: Can we at least organize a going away party?

MARIA: That would be so nice. . . . (*trails off.*)

EDUARDO: NO! We're leaving and we're not looking back. And if you dare try and use our names for your festival as some promotional device, I will formally and legally object. It was mine, not yours.

CATHERINE: It was ours, not yours.

EDUARDO: We'll have to agree to disagree.

HENRY: So, this is the end of a beautiful friendship.

EDUARDO: Yes, it is the end. (*Grabs MARIA*) Come on, we're leaving.

MARIA: (*To CATHERINE*) I'll stay in touch. On Facebook, maybe.

EDUARDO: No!

MARIA: You can't tell me who I can talk to and who I can't.

EDUARDO: Oh yes, I can! (*Grabs his violin case and gives it to MARIA*) Carry this. At least that's useful.

CATHERINE: (*Goes and gives MARIA a hug*) We still love you and your children. Don't forget the good times.

MARIA: I won't.

EDUARDO: (*Pulls MARIA away*) For God's sake, enough is enough. Let's get going. (*Stops and picks up a shot glass*) To a new life. To new friends, real ones! (*Downs the shot and throws the glass down*). Adios!

> *EDUARDO and MARIA exit. CATHERINE and HENRY finish the tequila in their glasses and start cleaning up the room.*

BLACKOUT

DETAILS, DETAILS, DETAILS!

CAST OF CHARACTERS

    O'REILLY: Late-fifties, well-dressed and articulate with no accent.

    GADLEY: Late-fifties, well-dressed, articulate, nervous and speaks fast.

    DELCAMPO: Late-forties, casually dressed, soft spoken, trace of a Southern accent.

    DEMOLINA: Late-thirties, well dressed, young looking and slender, a pronounced Spanish accent.

SETTING:

    The four are seated around a table in folding chairs. They are going through a big pile of papers, money, stocks, receipts and sorting them in piles. The conversation remains animated and there is frequent getting up to pour drinks from a side bar.

O'REILLY: I guess I started it all.

GADLEY: How so?

BY THE LETTER

O'REILLY: Well, the doctor wanders in to my office one day with his wife. Both are clueless, but he has a great financial future. They're looking to invest, so I sell them on the idea of some mutual funds and a couple of annuities.

DEMOLINA: Ah! So, that's where the infamous annuities started.

O'REILLY: Yes, a couple of annuities they could invest in over the years. (*Pauses*) How was I to know that the guy was also so stupid or naïve that he left his 401K entirely in bonds.

GADLEY: I heard this story.

O'REILLY: What exactly did you hear? I can only guess what he said because he calls one day and says he's changing his financial advisor to (*points to GADLEY*) you!

GADLEY: (*Points to himself*) Yours truly. (*Pauses*) So, this is what he tells me. The doctor and his wife stayed with you for a long time and keep pumping non-401K savings into your mutual funds and those annuities. Meanwhile, he keeps contributing the maximum amount to his 401K at his job. (*Swings his hands around*) He does this year after year as the stock market goes up and up and up. (*Pauses*) Then one day, he's talking with the clinic's executive secretary, an old lady who's worked there for years and who sees everyone's 401Ks, and she says, "Doctor, why do you have all your 401K money in bonds? You know you can choose other investments and you should certainly be investing in stocks at your age. Bonds are for old people like me. Most of your money needs to be in mutual funds. That's what's going up and up these days." (*Laughs*) And he says to her, "You mean I don't have to put all my 401K money into bonds?" "No," she says, "You can pick anything out of the big list of mutual funds and bonds so long as it stays within that particular company." And then he asks how he ended up in all bonds anyway and she says the CEO just put him there as a temporary expedient.

DELCAMPO: That "temporary expedient" lasted several years. Poor sucker.

O'REILLY: Jesus Christ! I had no idea! I never even asked how his 401K money was going.

GADLEY: Exactly! The good doctor comes and says to me, "I've been going to see this other guy (*points to O'REILLY*) for years and he never even asked me where or how I've been investing my 401K money. I must have lost thousands. The stock market never stopped going up." So, I answered that he might want to keep a few bonds and put the rest in mutual funds if he wasn't too risk adverse." And he yells "Risk adverse! Hell, no! I want every cent in the stock market from now on. My risk tolerance is sky high. No more bonds, ever!"

O'REILLY: It's true! I never asked him once about his 401K. I was so fixated on those annuities and my portfolio of investments that it didn't occur to me ask. I didn't think he was that stupid. Who would be putting all their money into bonds at his age. Totally naïve.

DEMOLINA: Naivety knows no bounds, but we'll get to that later. (*To O'REILLY*) So, what happened next?

GADLEY: (*Serves himself a drink*) I take a look at his portfolio and I move the mutual funds over to something from our company. And I suggest some things for him to do with his 401K that I can't touch anyway. But the best part was that he and his wife started some monthly auto-investment plan to the tune of a thousand dollars a month in a bunch of individual stocks. For a complete idiot, some of them were great investments. They were building up a fortune.

DELCAMPO: You never know, do you? They were always great savers.

GADLEY: No, you don't always know. (*Pauses*) So, I'm wracking my brains to figure out how I can make some money off this guy and I decide to sell him on the idea of managed account. "Let us make the investments and you pay a small percentage. You make money, I make money and we're all happy." (*Pauses*) I wondered if he was going to do it and then, miracle of miracle, he decides to give it a try.

BY THE LETTER

O'REILLY: I see what's coming.

GADLEY: Exactly! We take their stock portfolio, a nice chunk of change at that point, and we churn it and churn and churn it, selling everything, buying new stocks, selling those, buying others. It made their heads spin, literally. No way for them to keep track of anything. And in the end, we have a whole new portfolio under my care with a guaranteed little annual percentage that stays pretty much the same whether the damn account goes up or down.

O'REILLY: And I thought I was without scruples!

GADLEY: No, just without imagination.

DELCAMPO: Something happened to you, too. It must have, because they moved on.

GADLEY: No, I moved on. I'd had it with my company and I'd had it with this stinking state, so I just decided to move out. Not that I didn't propose to the doctor and his wife to stay with me and move their assets, but they decided to stay with the firm, so I left.

DELCAMPO: And that's when I came in.

GADLEY: Precisely!

DELCAMPO: I knew them through a mutual acquaintance. And I let that rotten fruit just fall from the tree into my hands. (*Pauses*) The weird thing is that I really liked them both, good people, very frugal and hardworking, very talented and sociable. In fact, they rebuilt their stock portfolio and continued to pump money into it. They were excellent savers, especially for a doctor and his wife. Plus, those annuities, of course, they just keep plugging along year after year, growing and growing.

DEMOLINA: Yes, the annuities. But we'll come to them later.

DELCAMPO: They really like me, too. I even helped the doctor put on an art show. (*Pauses*) Vanity was his real Achille's heel.

GADLEY: Isn't it all of our Achille's heels?

O'REILLY: (*Serves himself a drink*) I'd say greed if I had to pick.

DEMOLINA: No, I wouldn't really say that. It certainly wasn't the doctor and his wife. They give away too much money to be considered greedy. They had all sorts of charities, especially in the arts: museums, art programs, art schools, scholarships. It was really extraordinary.

DELCAMPO: That's true, very civic minded couple. (*Pauses*) Anyway, they really disliked that managed account model. Every time we talked it was "I don't understand the advantage to us. You make money whether the portfolio goes up or down." And stuff like that. He just didn't accept that the cost was offset by the improved gains.

GADLEY: Was it?

DELCAMPO: Sometimes, in the good years.

GADLEY: And in the bad ones? We had a few of those as I recall.

DELCAMPO: Well. . . not so much.

O'REILLY: Ha! Admit it! The doc was right! You made money whether the portfolio rose or fell, just a bit more when it was rising. So, what happened?

DELCAMPO: They finally decided to put their funds and their stocks in a different platform and I was asked if I wanted to continue with a fee-for-service model, just money for advice at a flat rate.

GADLEY: Did you? I never found those very useful or profitable. No money in that for me.

BY THE LETTER

DEMOLINA: That model is okay from time to time, especially if it leads to something more lucrative.

DELCAMPO: Yes, I did it for a few years until I got a different job and couldn't do independent financial consulting anymore.

O'REILLY: Conflict of interest?

DELCAMPO: No, just lack of time. It wasn't worth it to me anymore. I have a wife and young children and my salary was more than sufficient. I liked the doc and his wife, but not that much.

DEMOLINA: And then it was my turn.

O'REILLY: Where the hell did you come from?

DEMOLINA: Spain.

Q'QUINN, DELCAMPO and GADLEY: Spain?

DELCAMPO: Pretty good English for a foreigner.

DEMOLINA: Thanks.

O'REILLY: Where did you go to school?

DEMOLINA: *Instituto de Comercio de Barcelona*, The Commercial Institute of Barcelona. Graduated top of my class. But I always wanted to work in the United States, land of financial opportunity. Plus, my wife is American.

DELCAMPO: That doesn't explain how you met the doctor and his wife.

DEMOLINA: The internet, of course.

O'REILLY: You're kidding!

DEMOLINA: No, I'm not. I established a site that looks for expatriates from Spain and Latin American to assist them in financial planning and the doctor, who speaks excellent Spanish, stumbled across my site on the internet. It was a match made in heaven. *Una boda milagrosa*!

GADLEY: Yeah! I've had a few of those previous marriages. (*Gets DEMOLINA a drink*) They seemed to be made in heaven until they ended up in hell.

DELCAMPO: The doctor's no fool, nor is his wife. I'm sure they were skeptical of someone from the internet.

DEMOLINA: *Por supuesto*! Skepticism is natural, especially from his Columbian wife. But my innate Latin charm won them over little by little. Plus, I'm smart, articulate, personable.

GADLEY: And modest, too. (*Pauses*) Don't tell me! They signed over their accounts to you for full management and you churned them into butter and left them with a fiscal fiasco?

DEMOLINA: Of course not, the good doctor would not allow that, thanks to his previous negative experiences. (*Points to O'REILLY*) Once burned, twice cautious. (*Points to GADLEY and DELCAMPO*) Twice burned, thrice cautious.

GADLEY: Cute. (*Drinks*) Tell me about it. (*Raises his glass*) To my three former wives, may they rest in pieces.

DEMOLINA, DELCAMPO and GADLEY: Hear, hear!

DEMOLINA: So, I can't get a hold of the assets except that one little left-over part, a million dollars in annuities.

O'REILLY: Those annuities reached a million?

BY THE LETTER

DEMOLINA: Yes, and they were free and clear and ready to plucked.

GADLEY: I see what's coming, you little Latin devil.

DEMOLINA: They almost slipped through my fingers.

DELCAMPO: Do tell.

DEMOLINA: Yes! They were still with the same company where you (*points to O'REILLY*) put them. And then that stupid company goes and sells those annuities to another company without consulting any of the clients. They just transferred them to another company, plop!

DELCAMPO: So, it happens. Not nice, but not unusual either.

DEMOLINA: Well, the good doctor and his wife don't care for that, so I jump in and say, "Let's change them to another company where you get less fees, additional life insurance and better returns."

O'REILLY: And I have a bridge I can sell you in Brooklyn.

DEMOLINA: So, he asks "what's the down side?" And I answer, "the funds are blocked for six years."

GADLEY: That seems reasonable, especially if they don't need the money.

DEMOLINA: More than reasonable, *mi amigo*. They sign the papers, we transfer the annuities and I pocket $35,000 in commissions for a half a day's work.

DELCAMPO: With money out of the annuities?

DEMOLINA: No, of course not. That's the trade off, the company gets a million to work with for six years and I pocket $35,000 in commissions.

GADLEY: Sweet! You are a smart one.

DELCAMPO: Did you tell the doctor and his wife that was going to happen before they signed on the dotted line?

DEMOLINA: Hell, no! He might have held it up, especially since some jackass in our own company told them earlier that there was no advantage to switching the annuities anywhere.

DELCAMPO: Sound's like there wasn't.

DEMOLINA: Life insurance. They both get life insurance.

DELCAMPO: I remember the doctor let his life insurance lapse because it was too expensive at his age and they had enough money to live on without it.

O'REILLY: That would make sense. At some point, you really don't need it, do you?

DEMOLINA: Details, details!

GADLEY: $35,000 doesn't sound like a detail to me. It sounds like a hell of a lot of money.

DELCAMPO: The doctor and his wife didn't know?

DEMOLINA: Perhaps I failed to make it clear.

O'REILLY: Perhaps?

DEMOLINA: No, I think it slipped my mind.

DELCAMPO: Did it slip the good doctor's mind, too? What did he do when he got the first statement with a $35,000 commission?

DEMOLINA: (*Sighs*) He called and we chatted in Spanish.

BY THE LETTER

GADLEY: *Por supuesto*, as you say.

DEMOLINA: He questioned the sum and I assured him that it was not coming out of his account at all, but was paid by the company. He also asked if that meant he would be getting several years of free financial services in exchange, since he was paying annually for my services.

O'REILLY: Would he?

DEMOLINA: Of course not! I told him the two were completely different activities. He even asked if he had initiated the change of companies himself, would he have benefited from the commission?

DELCAMPO: Would he?

DEMOLINA: No! That particular firm does not deal with individual clients, just brokers.

GADLEY: Very convenient! I suppose that was on purpose, too?

DEMOLINA: Do you really expect me to answer that question?

DELCAMPO: So, what was the outcome?

DEMOLINA: I pocket the money, he has to wait another six years before he can touch it and if either of them dies, they get some life insurance.

O'REILLY: Do you think they'll stay with you as their trusted financial advisor after all that?

DEMOLINA: Why not?

O'REILLY, GADLEY and DELCAMPO: Why not?

DEMOLINA: (*Raises his hands*) I didn't do anything illegal.

O'REILLY: I didn't either, but I certainly did NOT put the client's welfare before my own. I just ignored his other investments. I just didn't care enough to get the whole financial picture.

GADLEY: Well, I acted in my own self-interest the whole way. I forced them into a managed care account and worked it until I couldn't pump anything out of it any more. Then I jumped ship. Off to greener and greener pastures (*holds up some money*). Get it? Greener and greener? (*Laughs.*)

> *O'REILLY, DELCAMPO and DEMOLINA all look at him laughing, but none of them join in.*

DELCAMPO: And I just couldn't justify the effort of dealing with them anymore. I put my wife and family before the client, seems normal somehow. We have to make choices in life.

DEMOLINA: (*Takes another drink*) I think you're all over reacting. The doctor and his wife and I established a bond, a good trusting working relationship. Then he gets hung up on a measly commission. It's positively petty.

DELCAMPO: I wouldn't call $35,000 a measly commission and certainly not petty.

DEMOLINA: So, what! We had an understanding, a mutual bond, cultural affinity. He would speak to me in Spanish and I indulged him. What more can you ask for?

O'REILLY: Transparency.

DELCAMPO: Loyalty.

GADLEY: Honesty.

DEMOLINA: Well, whatever happens, happens. *Que sera, sera*. But, I still have faith. I still have hope we can salvage our relationship.

DELCAMPO: I have hope, too, in wine! Hope for the truth in wine, *in vino veritas*.

DEMOLINA: What's that mean?

DELCAMPO: It's Latin. It means truth springs from wine. (*Raises his glass*) To truth!

ALL: To truth. (*Raise their glasses and all drink*).

DELCAMPO: To transparency, loyalty and honesty!

> *O'REILLY, GADLEY and DEMOLINA stare at DELCAMPO and none raises their glass.*

O'REILLY: What about to prosperity? (*Raises his glass*) To prosperity!

GADLEY: (*Raises his glass*) To prosperity!

DELCAMPO: (*Raises his glass*) Ours or the clients?

DEMOLINA: (*Raises his glass*) Details, details, details. (*Pauses*) To everyone's prosperity! Especially those in this room!

ALL: Hear! Hear! (*ALL raise their glasses and drink.*)

BLACKOUT

A TRIP TO FULTON, LOUISIANA

CAST OF CHARACTERS

>ERIC: Young man in his early thirties, eager and affable. Casually dressed.

>BARBARA: Eric's wife. In her mid-thirties. Attractive and articulate. Casually dressed.

SETTING

>A simple living room with a couch and a couple of worn chairs and a coffee table.

BARBARA: Fulton? Why would you want to drag us to Fulton?

ERIC: I have a job opportunity there.

BARBARA: It had better be damn good. I don't want to leave New Orleans and move to Central Louisiana unless we have to. Your family's here and so is mine.

ERIC: Maybe that's the problem. Sometimes I feel like I'm suffocating. (*Pauses*) Sure, I love the town and we have good friends, but how can I develop professionally if we stay here. Around here, everything's about who you know and how long your family has lived here.

BARBARA: That may be true, but it doesn't change a thing. At least you have family and job opportunities here. What will you have in Fulton?

ERIC: (*Stands and begins walking around the room*) They want a community organizer up there to work with the faith-based communities.

BARBARA: To do what?

ERIC: Whatever they want.

BARBARA: What's that supposed to mean.

ERIC: I mean that I get them organized together to accomplish goals on a community-wide scale, like improving housing, or getting better schools, or enacting police reform.

BARBARA: All of that?

ERIC: Maybe and maybe not.

BARBARA: Wasn't someone else already up there, some lady with a royal name? Princess? Or duchess? Or queenie? Or something like that?

ERIC: Yes, it was Marquise.

BARBARA: Yeah, Marquise. A great name. (*Pauses*) But she still didn't suceed up there.

ERIC: No, she didn't, but we will. She tried to tele-command things from Monroe, as I understand. But we'll make it happen right there in Fulton.

BARBARA: That town's a dump. There's nothing there at all, not even a decent university. Nothing but fast food joints and nail salons, plus a Wal-Mart.

ERIC: You're too harsh. They have a symphony, a museum and an art center, plus an historical museum and a zoo.

BARBARA: How much are they going to pay you?

ERIC: $24,000 a year.

BARBARA: That's ridiculous.

ERIC: Not up there. It's much cheaper up there than down here. Besides, it's the per capita income in the region, around $24,000 per year.

BARBARA: $24,000? That's half national average! That's poverty.

ERIC: Not quite, but close. (*Pauses*) We'll have enough. Remember, "Look to the lilies of the field, neither do they reap nor sow, but Solomon in all his glory was not arrayed like one of these."

BARBARA: Enough of the pontification. Save it for your ministerial alliance, if they really have one.

ERIC: I'm working on it. We have a few ministers and some rabbis and a priest or two.

BARBARA: That's the problem. You can't have an alliance with so few people. That place just won't support the kind of project you're proposing. Everyone, including Queenie/

ERIC: / Marquise.

BARBARA: Marquise, sorry. They've all failed and I'm afraid you will, too.

ERIC: Failure is not an option.

BARBARA: Failure is always an option, albeit not a desirable one. (*Pauses*) So when do you expect to go up there.

BY THE LETTER

ERIC: I'm going up for a couple of weeks for a trial project. Then we can move up there together a few months down the line.

BARBARA: And what do your parents have to say about this?

ERIC: What can they say, I grew up in ten towns before I was a teenager. We never stayed more than a few years anywhere. Now they're "settled" in New Orleans. It really doesn't matter what they think about any of it.

BARBARA: Maybe they're just worried about you and how it will work out.

ERIC: Maybe.

BARBARA: Maybe they don't want you to be disappointed.

ERIC: Maybe.

BARBARA: Maybe they don't want you so far away if and when we have children.

ERIC: Are you pregnant?

BARBARA: No, not yet, but it's always a possibility.

ERIC: We need to discuss that before you make a unilateral decision.

BARBARA: I'm a team player, remember?

ERIC: Speaking of team players, I just heard they fired Stephanie Harding.

BARBARA: Why?

ERIC: I don't really know, but she just took a sudden retirement.

BARBARA: Sounds fishy. She was one of the nicest, hardest working people I knew.

ERIC: Me, too. (*Pauses*) Someone wanted her out, I guess.

BARBARA: I wonder who?

ERIC: Every job has a cabal at the top. The attraction of power and money is irresistible.

BARBARA: Stephanie wasn't like that.

ERIC: No, she wasn't. And I think that upset the cabal, so they maneuvered her out whether she wanted to go or not.

BARBARA: Well, good for her. At least she will benefit from her retirement. (*Pauses*) They didn't take that away, did they?

ERIC: I don't think so. Not much they could do about that. Since she stayed on to help in the current crisis, they couldn't exactly fire her.

BARBARA: So, they maneuvered her out, right? I've seen it happen at our place.

ERIC: They probably created a new position and gave her the opportunity of applying for her own job, knowing that they had someone else in mind already.

BARBARA: Sounds plausible. (*Pauses*) Thank God you didn't take a job at that place. It could have been you. And I hope you won't get into a similar bind in Fulton.

ERIC: My boss up there is a saint. No one is in this work for the money, because there isn't that much. And the power is spiritual, not temporal. So, no one cares.

BY THE LETTER

BARBARA: Nice combination. No power, no money and a job that's likely to fail.

ERIC: Don't say that! If you don't believe in me, then who will?

BARBARA: (*Goes and caresses ERIC's hair*) Of course I believe in you. But I still worry about paying for groceries, paying for rent, getting health insurance and starting a 401K. You know what that is, right?

ERIC: (*Frowns*) Of course I do.

BARBARA: So, what's up there in Fulton, besides the Wal-Mart.

ERIC: Like I said, they have a museum and a symphony and several choirs. There's lots of hiking a outside activities in the national forest. There are even several theatre groups.

BARBARA: In that little town?

ERIC: Yes, I even heard about a developmental theatre group.

BARBARA: What's that?

ERIC: They write their own plays and put them on once a year. It's a ten-minute play festival.

BARBARA: Any good?

ERIC: I don't know. But I already got invited to be on the board.

BARBARA: How much is that going to cost you?

ERIC: Nothing, apparently. And I can submit an original play, direct one, and act in one or several if I have the time.

BARBARA: Aren't you supposed to be working up there?

ERIC: Of course, but we can still participate in community activities, build social capital and maybe hit the stage.

BARBARA: I thought you were over all that when you realized we were going to starve to death on your acting salary.

ERIC: Community organizing is like acting, just with a different audience.

BARBARA: Yeah, and a bunch of penniless priests and pastors that might pay you.

ERIC: Enough! We'll make this work as a team.

BARBARA: (*Begins to act*) Your Lordship (*bows*), may I welcome you to the Shire of Fulton in the wooded hills of Central Louisiana.

ERIC: (*Stands and takes her hand*) Your Ladyship, it is my pleasure to visit you in this terrestrial paradise where I hope to settle.

BARBARA: (*Looks around uneasily*) Well, I suppose you can use your imagination.

ERIC: Shall we dance?

BARBARA: With pleasure.

> *The music for Minet, a Czech Minuet, begins and they dance the choreographic version. ERIC and BARBARA are facing the audience with BARBARA on his right side. They do three waltz steps forward, three back, then the ERIC passes BARBARA from the right to the left. They repeat three waltz steps forward and three back and ERIC passes BARBARA to stand in front of him with her back to the audience. They do*

waltz steps in place while ERIC and BARBARA touch their hands right-to-right, then left-to-left, then right-to-right, and left-to-left. They hook right elbows and do four waltz steps to return to the side by side position. ERIC does four waltz steps, two towards the audience and two back to stand beside BARBARA. BARBARA does the same but ends up facing ERIC. They step to the side with the right foot, back with left, side with right in a grape vine step, ending with left to right. Then repeat in the opposite direction ending up face to face. ERIC and BARBARA repeat the right elbow hook and for waltz step in a clockwise direction and end up side by side facing the audience. ERIC and BARBARA bow to one another. Music ends.

ERIC: This was nice. It brings back a lot of good memories. Thank you.

BARBARA: My pleasure, Your Lordship.

ERIC and BARBARA sit down.

BARBARA: You know, I'm scared to go up there and not have it work out.

ERIC: Why?

BARBARA: Because we won't have any friends or relatives and you'll have an unstable job in a hostile environment. It might kill your self-confidence.

ERIC: (*Takes BARBARA in his arms*) We have our youth, our intelligence, our vision and we have each other.

BARBARA: It still scares me.

ERIC: (*Stands and pontificates*) "Even though I must walk through the valley of the shadow of death, I shall fear no evil." Remember that one?

BARBARA: I know. (*Pauses*) But I just don't have your self-confidence or faith.

ERIC: "He leads me in paths of righteousness for his name's sake." How about that one?

BARBARA: I know, I know.

ERIC: "The Lord is my shepherd, I shall not want."

BARBARA: Maybe you, but us? I want a stable home and a stable income and a loving family.

ERIC: (*Gives her a big kiss*) You have that. As long as we are together, then things will work out.

BARBARA: Even in Fulton, Louisiana?

ERIC: Even in Fulton, Louisiana.

BARBARA: Okay. I'll trust you.

ERIC: (*Points his finger at BARBARA*) But verify.

BARBARA: Right!

> *BARBARA takes ERIC in her arms and they embrace.*

BLACKOUT

DEFENESTRATION

CHARACTERS

    BEATRIX: High level administrator, plump, older middle-aged

    SHERRY: Slender, fast-talking older middle-aged woman

    DORIS: Subordinate to Beatrix, stocky, with a throaty voice

SETTING

    A non-descript office setting with a desk and a few chairs. A large portrait of an official hangs on the wall and an American flag sits in one corner.

    BEATRIX is seated in the desk and rises to great SHERRY as she enters. DORIS is seated in the other chair.

BEATRIX (*To SHERRY*) Sherry, so good to see you. Thanks for coming by. Have a seat.

DORIS: (*To SHERRY*) Hello, Sherry. How's your father doing?

SHERRY: (*Sits*) He died.

DORIS: (*Surprised*) I'm so sorry. I didn't know. I knew he was sick but no one ever told us that he died.

SHERRY: I kept it pretty quiet. No use upsetting other people.

BEATRIX: I believe I've already expressed my condolences.

SHERRY: Yes, thanks. It was a nice email.

DORIS: And your recovery?

SHERRY: I'm still limping a little, but it's getting better. At least I'm not in constant pain anymore.

BEATRIX: That was quite a nasty fall.

SHERRY: You bet! Slipping on a rug in my own house added insult to injury.

BEATRIX: So glad it wasn't at work. All that nasty paperwork.

SHERRY: Yes, the paperwork, of course. (*Pauses*) I still use a cane and it hurts at night, but I'll be okay. Working from my bed at home wasn't exactly ideal, especially with so many important things going on.

BEATRIX: Well, you did it.

DORIS: And we're so glad you could.

SHERRY: Thanks.

BEATRIX: Yes. (*Pauses*) So we're here to talk about the reorganization of your program. (*Pauses*) As you know, your program has gone from a modest budget of five million to a massive budget of 100 million dollars almost overnight.

DORIS: And not only do we have this huge influx of funds, there will be a huge corresponding increase in staff.

BEATRIX: Yes, fourteen positions at multiple levels.

SHERRY: That's really amazing! Are these full-time civil service jobs or contract positions.

DORIS: A mixture of contract and temporary jobs.

BEATRIX: With a few permanent positions in the central office, of course (*nods to DORIS*). (*Pauses*) We have to be prudent, of course, because who knows how long this federal largess will last.

SHERRY: So how do I fit into this new structure?

BEATRIX: Excellent question. (*To DORIS*) Doris?

DORIS: (*Long, awkward pause*) You don't.

SHERRY: I don't? What does that mean?

BEATRIX: Your position will cease to exist and there will be a higher position and some lower ones as well.

SHERRY: So, I will be moved into the higher position?

BEATRIX: No, but you could certainly apply and be considered for that job.

SHERRY: Apply for my own reconfigured position?

BEATRIX: Exactly.

SHERRY: Shouldn't I have the option of going straight into that higher position, even temporarily?

DORIS: That was considered.

BEATRIX: And rejected.

SHERRY: By whom?

BEATRIX: By the administration.

SHERRY: (*Looks skeptically*) Who exactly is "the administration?" I don't know anyone here by that name.

> *DORIS looks at BEATRIX and SHERRY follows her gaze to BEATRIX as well.*

SHERRY (CONT): I see. (*Pauses*) You know, I was eligible for retirement 18 months ago and I stayed to confront the current crisis.

DORIS: I know.

SHERRY: And I spent time away from my dying father to help out the department in a time of extreme need.

BEATRIX: And for that, we are eternally grateful.

SHERRY: Eternally grateful? And this is how I'm rewarded for my dedication? A chance to apply for my own position?

BEATRIX: It's not as bad as it sounds. You certainly stand a chance of being selected.

SHERRY: A chance! (*Pauses*) And who do you already have in mind, another one of your personal friends who wants a job advancement and a promotion for their retirement? Anyone I know?

BEATRIX: That's out of the scope of this discussion.

BY THE LETTER

SHERRY: (*To DORIS*) You agree with this? You think it's okay to treat loyal public servants who have devoted years of their lives to the department and the citizens of this state to just throw them away, especially during a crisis?

DORIS: We're not throwing you away. I still value your past contributions and I value your friendship.

SHERRY: Friendship! Friends don't treat friends like this. Friends show appreciation and compassion. They help one another and they don't throw one another under the bus or out the window.

BEATRIX: Let's not be overly dramatic. You'll still have your full retirement and be able to help with the transition of your future supervisor. After all, this is a complex organization with some very specific requirements. Your institutional knowledge will be invaluable to your successor.

SHERRY: A complex organization that I helped form and nurture and which continues whether I am there are not.

BEATRIX: Precisely. And from what I understood, the operations did continue during your absences, which could be a commentary on your role.

SHERRY: (*To DORIS*) Ah! My yearly evaluation! Now I understand. You wrote that things continued just as well with me as without me, which brought into question the necessity of my position. (*Pauses*) Now, I get it. It escaped me at the time but it was a set-up for subsequent removal. (*Points to BEATRIX and DORIS*) Clever girls.

DORIS: I'm sorry you take it that way.

SHERRY: How else am I supposed to take it. And you (*points to BEATRIX*) are the second level approver, so I guess you were already planning and plotting at that time.

BEATRIX: I'm not that Machiavellian.

SHERRY: Really? (*To DORIS*) What do you think, Doris? Is she that Machiavellian or not?

DORIS: Do you really expect me to answer that?

SHERRY: Of course not! It puts you in an awkward position and friends don't embarass friends, do they?

DORIS: Another rhetorical question, I suppose?

BEATRIX: (*To SHERRY*) So, what are your intentions?

SHERRY: I will not be applying for my own position.

BEATRIX: Well, that settles that.

DORIS: Will you stay around to help mentor your successor?

SHERRY: No! I'll be retiring in two weeks with two weeks of medical leave for emotional distress and much-needed rehabilitation.

DORIS: Can we at least organize a going away party?

SHERRY: NO!

DORIS: You have lots of good friends in the department.

SHERRY: And I'm sure they will reach out to me personally. (*Pauses*) No, this is it! No use prolonging this farce one day longer.

BEATRIX: I'm sorry you feel that way.

BY THE LETTER

SHERRY: Really? You get 100 million extra dollars, around a dozen new positions to pass around to your friends and acquaintances and you get the satisfaction of seeing me thrown out the window.

BEATRIX: (*Coolly*) Defenestration is the exact term.

DORIS: What does that mean?

SHERRY: They used to throw ministers they didn't like out the windows of a building in Prague.

BEATRIX: Out of the *hrad*, the official government building.

SHERRY: Exactly. You visited there as I recall. It must have been inspiring.

BEATRIX: Yes, I liked Prague. (*To SHERRY*) Do you have anything else to say?

SHERRY: I've said enough and I've seen enough.

DORIS: Can we still stay in touch?

SHERRY: I think that's a bad idea (*walks off stage*).

DORIS: That went poorly.

SHERRY: That went perfectly. We wanted her out and she complied. What more could your ask for?

DORIS: A little humanity. A trace of compassion.

BEATRIX: To govern, it is better to be feared than loved, remember?

DORIS: Machiavelli?

BEATRIX: Yes, and don't be talking about this with anyone. And don't get all teary-eyed and sentimental. This is a business, a multi-million-dollar business. Protecting the victims of internal abuse will only get you one place.

DORIS: Which is?

BEATRIX: Defenestrated, you fool! Thrown out the window. (*Pauses*) Let's go, we have more work to do.

BLACKOUT

COMMUNITY HEALTH

CHARACTERS

    MARTIN: Director of a small, rural family practice residency program. Middle-aged white man, no regional accent.

    PAXTON: Chief resident for the family practice residency. Mid-thirties. Somber and efficient.

    BARBARA: Executive secretary for the family practice residency. Cheerful, organized and a mother figure for the residents.

SETTING

    Non-descript office with a desk and a few chairs. Martin and Paxton are sorting through some papers while Barbara stands with a clipboard and a pen at the ready.

PAXTON: This one looks promising. Graduated from Nebraska and then went to St. Kitts. Seems like a good student with a good undergraduate education. MCATs are pretty good, too.

MARTIN: Black, white or Asian?

PAXTON: White, of course. (*Pulls another chart*) What about this one? East Indian name, from a great undergraduate school. Can't pronounce his name, but he was raised in the states, so he has to be fluent in English.

BARBARA: (*Takes the chart and reads*) "Abdendu Gujarati." Goes by "Abe" apparently.

MARTIN: You're good.

BARBARA: I've had a lot of practice. Either they are foreign-born, foreign-trained or American-born Caribbean school graduates, or American-born first-generation Asians. They all like it when I can pronounce their names correctly and don't shorten them, either.

MARTIN: No wonder they love you.

PAXTON: (*Takes another*) This one's from Mississippi, probably Black with that first name, and from a U.S. school. Something must be wrong with her.

MARTIN: (*Takes the folder*) Pretty low MCAT and near the bottom of her class. But she's Black and we certainly need the diversity. (*Hands the chart to BARBARA*) Put that one down on the list.

PAXTON: Anyone else?

MARTIN: Not today. I'm exhausted. (*Pauses*) I guess the good news is that we get a good crop every year. They're smart, usually well-off if their parents can send them to the Caribbean schools, or $500,000 in debt and desperate to finish up and get out there making big bucks. (*Pauses*) Are we done?

PAXTON: Not quite. We have to make some decision about the Community Health rotation.

MARTIN: What about it?

PAXTON: Have you seen the evaluations? Most of the students hate that doctor at the health unit. They say she's smart and articulate and a radical nut that forces her politics down their throats.

BY THE LETTER

MARTIN: Dr. Nugent?

PAXTON: Yes, Dr. Nugent. (*Takes another folder*) "Dr. Nugent makes us listen to hours of information about social justice and racism and the social determinants of health." (*Reads another*) This rotation is pure propaganda. I learned nothing except how Dr. Nugent went to medical school overseas in a foreign language and returned to hate America and American medicine." (*Takes another*) Or this one "Dr. Nugent has a vast knowledge and is obviously intelligent, but uses her intelligence to drag up rot about slavery and poverty and inequality, hardly the matter for medical students."

BARBARA: The students loved to work with her at the shelter. They all came back enthusiastic and fired up about public health. No one said anything bad about her at all. And she wrote a gracious thank you letter for their services.

PAXTON: That doesn't solve the problem of the Community Health rotation. That's the issue here, not the shelter work. Are we going to continue with that rotation or not?

MARTIN: I tried to reach out to her. I proposed a 2-week rotation with an emphasis on public health activities at the local and state level. I wanted her to focus on inspections, screenings and practical work, not theoretical political opinions. It needs to be about preventive medicine dealing with policy, not politics.

BARBARA: That sounds reasonable. And how did she respond.

MARTIN: (*Takes a letter*) "Your residents need to know about public health and community medicine. Hospitals are being reimbursed based on community (not just hospital) outcomes, a huge shift in policy and practice. I suspected some residents were unhappy and uncomfortable with some of the information imparted, something they were sometimes unwilling or unable to express (expect perhaps in their evaluations)."

PAXTON: Well, that's certainly the truth! They let her have it!

BARBARA: Did you share their concerns with Dr. Nugent?

PAXTON: Hell, no!

BARBARA: Wouldn't that be necessary to make things better?

MARTIN: (*Ignores the question*) It goes on: "Public health is unavoidably 'political' because it deals with population health, impacts of policy, comparative medical systems, historic injustice and social determinants of health. Sadly, these are not issues taught in a standard curriculum focused on health care delivery alone."

PAXTON: Damn right and a good thing, too!

MARTIN: (*Continues reading*) "These issues may also run afoul of some student's long-held conservative beliefs, a source of discomfort and irritation to them."

PAXTON: Well, she certainly got that right!

MARTIN: (*Continues reading*) "Shielding students from this information is, however, a disservice to their education. Those with an open mind and secure opinions reacted well, although they did not always agree. 'Pain is the breaking of the shell that encloses your understanding,' Kahlil Gibran."

PAXTON: What a pompous ass! That's insulting to you (*points to MARTIN*) and to me. We need to just eliminate that rotation all together. Pain, eh? You should show her some pain.

BARBARA: You already made Community Health an elective, so no one goes out to the health unit any more anyway. That's about the same, isn't it?

BY THE LETTER

MARTIN: There's more, "I was glad the residents got a taste of the medical shelter and I was grateful for their participation. That being said, I can't always guarantee a yearly hurricane."

PAXTON: What modesty! She can't guarantee a hurricane every year. Lord in heaven.

MARTIN: (*Continues*) "I do think that my interacting with the residents over a period of time convinced them that I did have something to offer, however difficult to stomach."

PAXTON: Well, it's makes me sick for sure.

MARTIN: Almost done: "It would be nice to have an honest, open discussion about this at your convenience. I know that student evaluations dictate decision making. That being said, I did not always like or agree with some of my professors (or colleagues), but I always learned something of use. Sharing the resident's feedback, however painful, can be helpful as well. I never based my evaluations on whether the resident appeared to agree or not, just their willingness to listen."

BARBARA: Isn't that true? Perhaps we could have shared some of the feedback? Dr. Nugent seems reasonable. What would be wrong with an honest discussion?

MARTIN: Just a bit more: "I also provided something of a disclaimer to the residents and a warning that some of the things they were going to learn might make them uncomfortable. Not sure that worked." (*Puts down the letter*) That's it.

PAXTON: A disclaimer didn't work for me or for most of the residents. Good riddance to this so-called doctor! Residents learn nothing, they get upset and it gives the residency a bad reputation. We work too hard to make them happy to have this self-righteous clown cause problems. (*To MARTIN*) So what did you decide?

MARTIN: I let Dr. Nugent know that I had moved past her proposed conversation.

PAXTON: Good!

MARTIN: And that her answer to my expression of my concern was not sufficient to alter the shape of the rotation and address the problems expressed by our residents. No change in her attitude, no rotation for our residents!

PAXTON: Good for you. Let her have it.

BARBARA: She didn't exactly say she wasn't going to change anything, just that the subject matter dictated her choice of material. I don't see what she could do exactly? Can she really just be quiet and eliminate all social commentary?

PAXTON: (*To BARBARA*) Why are you so concerned? This lady doesn't want to change. Our director (*points to MARTIN*) gives her an ultimatum and she turned it down. Case closed! To hell with her!

MARTIN: I still think Community Health offers a tremendous learning experience. But I'm the advocate for the concerns of the residents and that is what I always try and do.

BARBARA: By protecting them from views they don't agree with?

PAXTON: Come on, Barbara! You like everyone, you like the worst residents we have. You nurture them like little children. They call you "Mama" for God's sake. (*To MARTIN*) We have to run a serious program and get these kids ready for real-life medicine, not political correctness.

BARBARA: She wasn't teaching critical race theory, was she?

MARTIN: Pretty close. She showed maps where there were large slave populations and compared it with current county health rankings.

BY THE LETTER

BARBARA: Did it overlap?

MARTIN: A perfect overlap and that was 180 years ago. Pretty shocking.

PAXTON: Who cares! We're not teaching social justice. We're not raising saints or community health workers, we're training doctors, most of whom will go for the highest paying job they can get. They're all drowning in debt, except the ones from rich families. Why do they want to learn about the effects of poverty on health? They're only worried about their own poverty and its effect on their mental health.

MARTIN: (*To PAXTON*) Don't get excited. Barbara is just playing the devil's advocate, (*to BARBARA*) aren't you?

BARBARA: I've lived here all of my life and I hear the same things over and over about how poor people make bad decisions and that's why they have more sickness and death. And Dr. Nugent says it's related to poverty and low education and that poor people can't make the same choices. I've heard her talk. I've read her articles. None of the resident's complaints about her teaching should come as a big surprise.

PAXTON: Can we get back to the candidate selection? We've wasted enough time on Dr. Nugent and her crackpot ideas. We need to concentrate on serious medicine.

MARTIN: There won't be any more Community Health rotation, not as long as Dr. Nugent is there. She has some admirable qualities, but she's just out of touch. I don't know a single doctor around here that agrees with anything she says. We need to train our residents for the real world, not some hypothetical paradise.

BARBARA: So, that's why we don't see any Medicaid patients?

PAXTON: Just the ones we can't avoid to take, you know that. We're not training doctors for the indigent population, not if they have to make any money. We're training them from profitable practices in upscale locations, if they can find them.

BARBARA: Don't you want them to stay around here and increase the pool of family doctors.

MARTIN: That would be nice, but this is a poor, poorly educated and unhealthy area with an army of plaintiff's attorneys. More like a hell than a paradise. (*Pauses*) But some will stay and God bless them.

BARBARA: (*To MARTIN*) Is there anything else you need from me?

MARTIN: I think that's it. (*Pauses*) And please don't share any of this with Dr. Nugent, I know you see her in some artistic circles.

BARBARA: Of course not. (*Gathers up some papers and exits.*)

PAXTON: Watch out for her. She might have a little red streak, too. Artistic circles, indeed.

MARTIN: Oh, shut it! Barbara's a saint. Looking after the residents, especially the weak ones, the unstable ones, the insecure ones. They love her to death. A bit like Dr. Nugent.

PAXTON: Who loves her? Not our residents.

MARTIN: Didn't you hear, she was named Person of the Year for this entire area by a regional publication.

PAXTON: You've got to be kidding.

MARTIN: Nope, Person of the Year. She was praised for her work in public health and support of the arts. (*Pauses*) And she's too radical to teach our residents. Kind of weird, isn't it? Maybe it's more of a reflection on us then on her.

BY THE LETTER

PAXTON: That's crap! She'll be dead and gone and our students will be scattered all over this state and the nation. No one will remember her at all. Her social justice and racial inequity, her social determinants of health will die with her and this place will go on just as it always has. (*Picks up another folder*) What about this one, name looks Hispanic, maybe Mexican, and a woman, too. Might be good for diversity.

MARTIN: Of course, we need to be socially correct.

> *MARTIN and PAXTON chuckle as they toss the folders on to the table.*

BLACKOUT

KATIA AND THE DEVIL

Adapted from a Czech Folk Tale by David Holcombe

CHARACTERS

>NARRATOR
>KATIA
>LITTLE DEVIL
>LUCIFER
>SHEPARD
>KING
>ASTROLOGER
>QUEEN
>VARIOUS VILLAGERS
>VARIOUS PALACE GUARDS AND ATTENDANTS
>OTHER DEVILS

The size of the cast depends on how many children need to be included.

SET

A simple set since the interactions occur in various locales. No complex set requirements.

NARRATOR: Katia was a lovely Czech girl. She lived in a thatched-roof cottage and even had a little money to her name. She was hard-working, but she was so loud-mouthed that none of the village boys would have anything to do with her.

KATIA: I'm so cute! I'm hard working! So, what if I'm a little loud? So, what if I scream? Everyone has their problems in this world.

NARRATOR: One Sunday afternoon, she went into the village to the inn where the villagers were dancing. Katia could only look on because no one would ask her to dance.

> *The villagers can dance to any number of short Czech dances such as Svecovsky or Volky.*

KATIA: (*Addressing the audience loudly*) I swear that today I would dance with the devil himself if he came through that door.

> *LITTLE DEVIL appears. Everyone stops and watches in amazement. He walks straight to KATIA and bows and speaks to her.*

LITTLE DEVIL: Oh, beautiful Katia, would you please dance with me?

> *The music resumes with a polka and KATIA and the LITTLE DEVIL dance, first alone, and then everyone joins in. When the dance ends, KATIA and the LITTLE DEVIL go downstage. KATIA hangs on to the LITTLE DEVIL.*

KATIA: (*Screaming*) Dear stranger, you're a great dancer. If only I could be with you forever.

LITTLE DEVIL: Nothing easier, Katia, my dear. Just hold on to me and I'll take you to my home. We can dance there together forever.

KATIA: Where do you live?

LITTLE DEVIL: You'll find out. Just hang on to me.

NARRATOR: So off they flew together to Lucifer's Kingdom.

> *The villagers exit and LUCIFER enters, surrounded by a multitude of little devils. LUCIFER sit on a throne, brought in by the little devils.*

OTHER DEVILS: Look at this? Look what Little Devil has brought to us. What a pretty girl.

LITTLE DEVIL: This is Katia from the Czech village of Kolin. She's a good dancer, but is she loud. Help me unload her.

> *The other devils try and detach KATIA who hangs on to LITTLE DEVIL at all cost. They pull and tug, but KATIA will not let go.*

LUCIFER: (*Stands and holds up his pitchfork to stop the agitation*) Who have you brought here among us?

LITTLE DEVIL: (*Bows respectfully and points to KATIA who is still hanging on*) Great King Lucifer, I have brought you Katia from the village of Kolin. She wanted to dance with me forever and now she won't let go.

LUCIFER: Fool! You can't even follow simple instructions. You must pick your victims more carefully. Katia has a big mouth, but she's an honest, hard-working peasant girl. This is no place for her. Take her back and figure out how to get her off you. (*Waves his pitchfork*) GO! (*Returns to his throne.*)

> *LITTLE DEVILS remove the throne and exit the stage.*

BY THE LETTER

NARRATOR: The Little Devil took Katia back to her village, but he could still not get rid of her. He promised her wealth, beauty, fame and a long life, but Katia just giggled and refused to let go. Finally, the Little Devil went to see a wise shepherd to ask for help.

> *A SHEPHERD in a sheepskin coat watches over his sheep in a simple setting with a tree or two.*

LITTLE DEVIL: Hello, good shepherd? How are you doing?

SHEPHERD: (*Looks at KATIA hanging on to the LITTLE DEVIL's arm*) I'm fine, thanks, but what's that you're dragging around?

LITTLE DEVIL: Oh, it's nothing, just Katia from Kolin. I was just minding my own business when she came up and grabbed me and now she won't let go. (*Imploringly*) Can you please help me?

SHEPHERD: Sure, but you'll have to watch my sheep for me. (*Motions to KATIA*) Katia from Kolin, come grab me instead.

> *KATIA transfers over to the SHEPHERD, grabbing his sheepskin coat. He takes off the coat and deposits it and KATIA on to the ground.*

SHEPHERD (CONT): There, Katia, just sit down awhile.

LITTLE DEVIL: Thank you, kind Shepherd. Someday I will make you a rich man. But know now that I am a devil.

SHEPHERD: If all devils are such fools, then the world has nothing to fear from them.

> *SHEPHERD, LITTLE DEVIL and KATIA exit. The ASTROLOGER, KING and QUEEN enter the stage. It is the royal court.*

NARRATOR: Bohemia was ruled at this time by a rich and wicked king and queen. They imposed heavy taxes and wasted the people's money on idle pleasures. One day, they decided to ask the court astrologer to read their future in the stars.

KING: Astrologer, come here! I want you to read the future for the queen and I in the stars.

ASTROLOGER: (*Bowing low*) Your Highness, I have already seen the future, but I dare not speak.

KING: Speak! I command you! But remember that if it does not come to pass, you will pay with your life.

ASTROLOGER: Sire, I fear you have spoken rashly, but if I must, I will speak. (*Pauses*) It is written in the stars that at the end of this month, the devil will come for you both.

KING and QUEEN: What!

QUEEN: The devil is coming for us both?

KING: Guards! Come take him away and throw him in prison. If he is wrong, he will die. If he is right (*pauses*) than we may die. (*Turning to the royal entourage*) Leave us alone at once!

QUEEN: (*When they are alone*) Sire, let us change our ways and rule wisely. Perhaps if we are good and kind to the people, the devil will leave us alone.

KING: (*Nods in agreement*) Maybe we can try.

NARRATOR: So, the King and Queen changed their ways. They began to rule the land with wisdom and justice. The taxes were used for the good of the country and not for their selfish pleasures. Meanwhile, the

BY THE LETTER

Little Devil returned to the Shepherd in order to fulfill his promise to make him a rich man.

> *SHEPHERD and LITTLE DEVIL enter stage left and speak to one another.*

LITTLE DEVIL: Shepherd, listen to me. At the end of the month you must go to the royal palace. I will come to get the King and Queen. When I come for the Queen, you stand in front of her and say "Devil be gone, if not, you will have trouble!" I will leave her and she will surely reward you well. But when I ask for the King, do not interfere. He is mine.

SHEPHERD: I will be there and do as you say.

NARRATOR: And so, it came to pass that at the end of the month, the King and Queen waited in terror at the palace, surrounded by their loyal citizens.

> *The setting is the Royal Palace with the KING and QUEEN surrounded by a crowd, including the SHEPHERD. KATIA is inconspicuously at the back of the crowd.*

KING: It has been a month. The devil will come today or he will not come at all. Bring in the Astrologer.

ASTROLOGER: (*Enters and bows*) Your Highness, the Devil will surely come. It has been written in the stars.

QUEEN: But we have been good and virtuous. We have ruled with wisdom and kindness. Surely, we will be spared?

LITTLE DEVIL: (*Enters and walks up to the QUEEN*) Good day, You Majesty, you look lovely today. Are you ready to come with me?

SHEPHERD: (*Steps forwards and points to the LITTLE DEVIL*) Devil, be gone. Leave this virtuous woman or you will have trouble.

LITTLE DEVIL: (*Pretending to be afraid*) Oh, great shepherd. I must obey you. The Queen will be spared.

QUEEN: (*Very relieved*) Thank you, good shepherd, you have saved my life. Take these sacks of gold and jewels as a gift to you.

> *Servants present several heavy sacks to the SHEPHERD.*

LITTLE DEVIL: (*Turns to the KING*) As for you, wicked King, your only pretended to be virtuous and secretly continued your evil ways. You are not so lucky. Come with me for your just rewards.

KING: Shepherd, please save me! You will have a castle full of gold as your reward. Save me!

LITTLE DEVIL: (*To SHEPHERD*). Remember, do not interfere. You have promised and he is mine.

SHEPHERD: Devil, be gone! You need not fear me, but Katia still wants to dance with you.

> *KATIA bursts out of the crowd. The LITTLE DEVIL flees in horror with KATIA in hot pursuit. The crowd bursts out in cheers and clapping.*

KING: Thank you, good shepherd. You will have your castle and your gold. The Astrologer will tend your sheep instead of the stars. Let's celebrate with a dance.

> *KATIA returns alone and the LITTLE DEVIL has gotten away. She dances with the*

BY THE LETTER

SHEPHERD and the whole entourage join in a final dance, Studanka from Pilsen.

BLACKOUT

THE HOUSE ON SAVA STREET (PORTRAIT OF A FAMILY IN NINE HOLIDAYS)

(Revised 20 September, 2020)

CHARACTERS (IN ORDER OF APPEARANCE)

KEVIN: Jacob, Heather, Daniel and Wanda's father. Older man with some arthritic issues. Victoria's husband. Intelligent and patient. Down to earth. Friendly.

VICTORIA: Jacob, Heather, Daniel and Wanda's mother. Kevin's wife. Older woman in good shape. Talented but unrealistic. Loving.

WANDA: Jacob, Heather's and Daniel's younger sister. Kevin and Victoria's youngest daughter. Larry's wife and Martin's mother. Jovial, light-hearted and superficial. Brash and opinionated.

LARRY: Wanda's husband and Martin's father. Quiet and reserved. Patient.

MARTIN: Wanda and Larry's son. Taciturn. Intelligent.

HEATHER: Daniel, Jacob and Wanda's sister. Kevin and Victoria's older daughter. Clipped speech. Very direct to the point of being abrasive.

BY THE LETTER

DANIEL: Heather, Wanda and Jacob's sibling. Insecure as a youth, but arrogant and pompous as an adult. Intelligent but lacking empathy.

JACOB: Heather, Daniel and Wanda's older brother. Sophia's husband and Dylan's father. Articulate and pompous. Underlying insecurities.

SOPHIA: Jacob's wife and Dylan's mother. Reserved, intelligent and suspicious. Feels more at ease with the dead than the living.

DYLAN: Jacob and Sophia's son. Flighty and quick to anger. Intelligent. Unpretentious.

NOTE TO THE DIRECTOR: The characters age during the course of the play. Their personality traits remain about the same, but their physical appearance may change over time.

BRIEF SYNOPSIS

An American family interacts through a series of holiday gatherings. Issues of sibling rivalry, hypocrisy, racism, sexuality and death highlight each of the nine holidays, which may be played independently. If played together, the order must be respected. All scenes take place at Kevin and Victoria's home on Sava Street.

TABLE OF CONTENTS

THE HOUSE ON SAVA STREET (PORTRAIT OF A FAMILY IN NINE HOLIDAYS)

ACT I
- SCENE I: THANKSGIVING (SIBLING LOVE) 188
- SCENE II: EARTH DAY (PROSPERITY) 198
- SCENE III: HALLOWEEN (INSIGHT) 209
- SCENE IV: COLUMBUS DAY (UNFAIR ADVANTAGE) 217

ACT II
- SCENE I: GOOD FRIDAY (BURYING BARBIE) 228
- SCENE II: FATHER'S DAY (ONLY OUR DNA) 241
- SCENE III: DAY OF THE DEAD (PEACEFUL REPOSE) 250

ACT III
- SCENE I: CHRISTMAS (MAKING WREATHS) 261
- SCENE II: NEW YEAR'S DAY (THE HOUSE ON SAVA STREET) ... 271

BY THE LETTER

SETTING

> KEVIN and VICTORIA's home on Sava Street. It is divided into three segments: A central dining room, a den on the right and a garden on the left. There is a large table in the middle of the dining room, which can be represented by blocks joined together. There is a low wall (or several blocks) that separates the stage into the formal dining room and the den. The den can have a sofa and some chairs and a coffee table, also represented by portable black cubes. Part of the stage left represents a garden with a bench (or two black cubes). All set elements can be simplified and suggestive and need not be overly realistic. Blocks can be used to represent furniture and also serve as places where actors can stand to deliver some lines. A more realistic set can be used at the director's discretion.

ACT I

SCENE I

THANKSGIVING (SIBLING LOVE)

KEVIN wipes the sweat off his forehead and brushes back his hair before grabbing a card table (or black cube) and pulling it into the den. He sets it down in that room. VICTORIA is at a large dining table in the dining room where she is putting out place mats.

KEVIN
Is that where you want it?

VICTORIA
(*Surveys the position and points over to the right*) Move it over there so it will be in the middle of the room. We'll need four folding chairs, of course.

KEVIN
(*Goes off stage left and returns with a couple of chairs in each hand and places them around the card table*) You know it's always a problem to decide who sits in this room and who gets to sit at the big table in the dining room.

BY THE LETTER

VICTORIA
A problem? Why?

KEVIN
Because Wanda always complains that she and Larry and Dylan have to sit in here while everyone else gets to sit with the grown-ups at the big table (*points over to the other big table in the dining room.*)

VICTORIA
(*Stops putting placemats on the big table and comes over to listen. Folds her arms across her chest*) You're just exaggerating.

KEVIN
You know as well as I do that no one wants to sit out here and Wanda always wonders why we are punishing her.

VICTORIA
Punishing! Who says anything about punishment? It's just a card table and it's only a few feet from the rest of us. That's ridiculous. It just can't be that big a deal.

KEVIN
Apparently, it IS a big deal, at least to her. We go through this same discussion every Easter, Mother's Day, Thanksgiving and Christmas. Wanda gets stuck out here in the den with her family and she feels left out.

VICTORIA
Yes, and when we put Wanda and Sophia at the same table, they always manage to get into a fight about something or other. It doesn't even matter about what. It can be politics, money, immigration or schools. You'd think those two really disliked each other, even if they are sisters-in-law.

KEVIN
Especially because they're sisters-in-law, I would say.

VICTORIA
And don't forget the tablecloth. Please use the white one with the crocheted border.

KEVIN goes off stage left and returns with the tablecloth, which he spreads over the table (or cubes.)

KEVIN
And what if we put the card table at the end of the big table in the dining room? That way we would make one big table and be together in the same room.

VICTORIA
You know we're not going to start moving all the furniture around just because two grown women can't seem to get along. (*Pauses*) And use the good placemats out here, too. Just like the ones I'm using in the dining room. We don't want anyone to feel left out, do we? (*VICTORIA hands KEVIN some place mats.*)

KEVIN
So who's going to be the fourth person out here?

VICTORIA
What about Dylan? He and Martin are cousins, after all. He's quite a bit younger than Wanda and Larry, but only a bit older than Martin. I think he might add something to the conversation.

KEVIN
Dylan and Wanda don't get along either, even if she's his aunt. Plus, Martin is very intelligent, but he's awkward and doesn't talk much. I don't think any of them like each another, even if they're related. (*Pauses*) We're sociable people, nice people, with lots of friends and our kids are indifferent or even hostile to each other. It's amazing. I don't know where they got that. They don't have a shred of sibling affection.

BY THE LETTER

VICTORIA hands KEVIN the plates.

VICTORIA
Of course they love one another. They're family, right? And families are supposed to get along together through thick and thin, just like us.

KEVIN
We've had our share of problems, but we're still married, like Wanda and Larry and Sophia and Jacob. Everyone else is just related. I guess we can't make people love one another or even like one another for that matter, even if they're our children. (*Finishes putting silverware*) Honey, can't we move everyone to the big table, please? Just this time to see how it goes?

VICTORIA
No!

KEVIN
For peace and harmony's sake?

VICTORIA shakes a fork in his direction.

VICTORIA
You talk like we're a bunch of animals fighting in a barnyard. The children may have their differences, but in the end, they all love one another.

KEVIN
No, dear, they don't! And I shudder to think of what will happen when we're gone, despite our precautions. (*Picks up a couple of forks and begins banging them together like sabers*) They'll fight over every fork, every spoon, every glass and every piece of worthless furniture, not to mention the house itself. (*Gestures toward VICTORIA with a fork and holds it in the air like a sword*) En garde! I want that dining room table, and I'll fight for it. En garde! (*Clicks the forks in a mock battle.*)

VICTORIA

Stop it! Put those forks down. You'll stab someone by accident. (*Pauses*) No! They won't fight over everything because we've made the necessary arrangements.

> *Removes the forks from KEVIN's hands and replaces it on the table. VICTORIA sits down on one of the chairs and KEVIN sits down on the adjacent chair.*

VICTORIA (CONT)

What did we do wrong?

KEVIN

Nothing.

VICTORIA

We have to have failed somewhere. Children are supposed to love and support one another. (*Gestures at the table*) It can't be because of this, being at the big table or the small one, can it? We've treated them all the same.

> *KEVIN shrugs and reaches out to take VICTORIA's hand.*

KEVIN

Maybe we have treated them all the same. And maybe that was the problem; we should've treated them differently. They're certainly very different from one another.

VICTORIA

I'll say!

KEVIN

And maybe we just didn't know which table to put them at for Thanksgiving.

BY THE LETTER

VICTORIA

(*Stands up*) No! We've always done our best. We've been loving, supportive parents and our children have wanted for nothing, especially love.

The doorbell rings. KEVIN walks over and opens a door stage left. WANDA stands there with a bouquet of flowers. WANDA kisses KEVIN and goes over and kisses VICTORIA.

WANDA

Hello, Dad. Hello, Mom. I just thought I'd drop some flowers by for dinner. (*Hands VICTORIA a fall-themed bouquet. Glances from the small table to the big table in the living room*) Let me guess. Larry and Martin and I will be sitting at the small table in the den? And perhaps with Dylan?

WANDA goes over and sits down on one of the folding chairs. VICTORIA and KEVIN do the same.

VICTORIA

These are lovely flowers; I adore the fall foliage and the chrysanthemums, so autumn looking. (*Points to the large table*) Don't you think the table looks nice?

WANDA

Yes, it looks fine, it's just that it's a little annoying to be stuck here at the little kid's table while the adults are over there (*points at the big table*) at the big table having fun. How do you think that makes me feel? Or Larry or Martin? We feel like the unwanted distant relations or the children at the kid's table.

WANDA stands up and begins gesticulating.

WANDA (CONT)
I love to come over here. We appreciate you hosting these family get-togethers. I know it's a lot of time and work and money. But can't you put Jacob and Sophia or Heather at the card table and let my family and I sit at the big table? Just for once? Put someone else here (*points to the card table*) for once! (*Raises her voice*) Anyone but us!

KEVIN
Don't yell at your mother.

WANDA sighs and sits down.

VICTORIA
You and Sophia don't seem to have much in common. When you're together at the big table, there's always so much fussing and fighting.

WANDA
Much in common? That's a joke. Sophia's always pontificating about child rearing or medicine or some important genealogical meeting where she's going to discuss dead people. She doesn't talk, she lectures. It's boring and it's annoying. Put them at the little table, just once. Put Sophia and Daniel here with Dylan at this table. Let them be one small happy family out here, talking about intellectual topics of historical interest, and the rest of us can sit at the big table and just have fun. That would solve the problem, wouldn't it?

VICTORIA
But we can't.

WANDA
Why not? Because you love and respect them and you don't love or respect me and my family, or care what we think or feel? Is that it? Don't our feelings count at all?

BY THE LETTER

VICTORIA

Of course they do! We love you all. And we want you to love one another. We want a loving family where everyone gets along without fighting or criticizing or yelling.

KEVIN

(*To VICTORIA*) Please, don't upset yourself.

VICTORIA

I'm not upsetting myself. She's upsetting me (*points to WANDA*).

WANDA stands up.

WANDA

So that's it. I'm the one. I'm the problem child. (*Walks toward the door*) Okay, we'll sit in the den at the little table again. I'll make the sacrifice for the sake of the greater good. (*Points to the card table*) We'll sit here and we'll pretend to love everyone and be happy and we won't fight. Is that what you want? (*Checks her watch*) We'll be back at seven with our good clothes and our best manners. But don't expect me to smile and act like we're really happy about it. That's asking too much.

KEVIN stands up to see WANDA out.

KEVIN

We want you to be happy. And we love all of our children equally.

WANDA

Yes, just like in Animal Farm. You love all of your children equally; you just love some more equally than others.

VICTORIA stands up, knocking her chair over in the process.

VICTORIA

No! It's not like that at all. Some children are just needier than others.

WANDA

That's supposed to make me feel better? (*Pauses*) So do the needier children get to sit at the big table or at the kid's table?

> *VICTORIA begins to answer, but KEVIN raises his hand.*

KEVIN

Don't answer that!

WANDA

I can take it. I'm a big girl.

KEVIN

We love you all, and we look forward to seeing you later this evening. Thank you for bringing the beautiful flowers. It's a lovely gesture and we really appreciate it.

WANDA

Can we have at least one flower in a bud vase at the kid's table, or is that asking too much?

VICTORIA

There'll be flowers on both tables. I'll split the bouquet. It'll be fine.

WANDA

I guess I should be thankful for that.

> *WANDA opens the door and sees herself out. KEVIN returns to the table and picks up the overturned chair. KEVIN and VICTORIA both sit down.*

KEVIN

Can we move this table over and put it next to the big one now? I know it'll be crowded, but I can't live through another scene like that.

BY THE LETTER

VICTORIA

Yes, I think that would be a good idea. (*Sighs*) Let's hope the conversation doesn't get into politics.

KEVIN

Why not? Nothing like a good spirited political discussion to warm up the house.

KEVIN takes VICTORIA's hand.

KEVIN (CONT)

Let's move the tables together, please.

VICTORIA

Okay. But I'm still not happy about it.

KEVIN

Happiness is a by-product of a life well lived, not a goal. Let's move this darn thing.

KEVIN and VICTORIA move the card table next to the big table and begin arranging the place mats and chairs.

BLACKOUT

SCENE II

EARTH DAY (PROSPERITY)

SETTING

>Kevin and Victoria's home. Wanda uses the dining room and den side of the stage.

>>WANDA *has a large box filled with things to set the dining room table. WANDA pulls out and spreads a faux Provençal tablecloth on the dining room table. She distributes matching red placements and a set of dishes from Pottery Barn. WANDA frames each plate with silverware and adds the water and wine glasses. There is a fall themed floral arrangement, which complements the red and yellow color scheme. A single shaft of intense sunlight shines from the garden and illuminates the table. WANDA steps back to admire the effect. The front door opens and shuts.*

>>LARRY

I'm here. (*Enters stage right.*)

>>WANDA

In the dining room! Come see.

BY THE LETTER

LARRY
(*Peeks into the dining room and examines the table*) Very nice. I need a drink.

WANDA
Sure.

> *WANDA goes to the side bar and removes a bottle and two glasses. She pours two drinks. LARRY sits on a couch in the den. LARRY starts to prop his heels onto the coffee table, but stops and sets them back on the floor.*

WANDA
So how was your day?

LARRY
Where did all that new stuff on the dining room table come from? I've never seen it before. Does it belong to your folks?

WANDA
What stuff?

LARRY
The dishes, the tablecloth, the glasses, the flowers, the vase.

WANDA
Don't be upset. It was all on sale, fifty percent off at Pottery Barn. I couldn't resist. (*Pauses*) It'll be a big surprise for Mom and Dad when they get back. Just a little thank you gift for letting us use their home for the evening.

> *LARRY takes a huge gulp from his glass and WANDA does the same.*

LARRY
Your mom and dad don't need a goddamn thing. They have a house full of stuff and they really don't want anything more. We're just over here for a meal to celebrate Martin's birthday because you're ashamed of our house. That's all. I know you said you were going to prepare dinner, but all this! (*Shakes his head*) I don't get it. (*Pauses*) Do you know how much money I made today?

WANDA
No.

LARRY
Two hundred dollars, maybe not even that.

WANDA
(*Pointing to the table*) It didn't cost that much, I swear. Mom will really appreciate the gesture. I know she will. They do so much for us, you know that.

LARRY
We're broke. I'm not making enough money. We can't pay the mortgage. And you're buying a bunch of crap from Pottery Barn for your parents. For heaven's sake, what are you thinking?

WANDA
It's Martin's eighteenth birthday. He's inviting his girlfriend over so we can meet her and so can Mom and Dad. Can we at least make a nice impression?

LARRY
Which girl friend? He's had a dozen.

WANDA
Emma. She's very pretty, super intelligent and extraverted, a nice girl, and Martin really likes her.

BY THE LETTER

LARRY
He's eighteen. He's going to have a bunch of girl friends in college. Speaking of college, did he finally choose a school?

WANDA:
He'd like to go to Columbia.

LARRY
He can't go to Columbia.

WANDA
Why?

LARRY
Because they only offer partial scholarships.

WANDA
Maybe we can. . . . (*trails off.*)

LARRY
What? Stop eating? Borrow more money? With what collateral? We already owe more on our house than it's worth. (*Finishes off his glass with one gulp*) He has to go to an in-state school, the closer the better. He doesn't have any choice. (*Pauses*) We don't have any choice. It's got to be a state school, if he can get into one. The competition's fierce nowadays.

WANDA
He's smart! No, he's brilliant. I'm sure he'll get into any school he wants, instate or out. (*Pauses*) And what if I got a job?

LARRY
What job?

WANDA
Any job. I saw they were looking for cashiers at the Super One.

LARRY

And who's going to drive Martin to debate team after school, and tutoring, and whatever else he does?

WANDA

He could drive himself.

LARRY

How? We can't afford insurance for him. It's over $700 dollars for six months. We're broke and you're buying dishes for your parents just to impress his girlfriend. I need another drink.

WANDA takes his glass and stands up and then goes to the bar and pours another drink. The front door bell rings. WANDA delivers the drink to LARRY, who sits motionless on the couch and then goes to the front door and opens it. MARTIN stands in the doorway.

WANDA

(*Hugs MARTIN and kisses him*) You look great.

MARTIN goes in and sits in one of the two chairs facing the couch.

WANDA

Where's Emma? It thought she was coming so we could meet her.

LARRY

Yeah, we were looking forward to meeting her and introducing her to your grandparents.

MARTIN

She just got accepted to Columbia, my dream school.

WANDA

That's wonderful for her. (*Looks from MARTIN to LARRY*) Something to drink? A coke? Orange juice?

MARTIN

Orange juice, please, as long as it's organic.

WANDA

(*Hesitates*) Organic? I don't really know if it is. Organic's usually twice as expensive. (*Pauses*) Since when have you gone organic?

MARTIN

Emma always uses organic. She says everything's so full of pesticides and hormones these days.

LARRY

Emma in Columbia, eh? That's terrific. I know you want to go there, too, but I think you're going to have to stay closer to home, at a state school.

WANDA

That's too bad. It would be so cool if you could both go to Columbia. (*Turns to MARTIN and puts her hand on his knee*) Wouldn't it?

MARTIN

(*Answers in an emotionless monotone*) Yeah, that would be cool. But it's not practical.

> *WANDA goes and hurries back with a glass of orange juice. WANDA hands the glass to MARTIN.*

WANDA

I think it's organic. (*Turns to LARRY*) Another scotch?

LARRY

(*Shoves his glass in WANDA's direction*) That would be great, thanks.

WANDA returns to the bar and pours two more generous scotch and waters and returns to the group.

MARTIN

Emma's parents always wanted her to go to Stanford, but she said that seemed so pretentious. And she couldn't bear to go anyplace that wasn't a thousand miles from here. So, Columbia seemed like a great choice for her, and for me.

WANDA

It's a bit pricey.

MARTIN

It's only $46,000 tuition a year, plus room and board, of course, and travel costs. For such a prestigious school, Emma says that's a real bargain. At least that's what her parents say. (*Pauses*) Even though it costs a bundle, her parents say it's worth it, if only for the networking possibilities. (*Pauses*) But I know I couldn't go there even if I were accepted.

WANDA

Oh, I don't know. It might be a stretch, but we could possibly manage.

WANDA looks over at LARRY for some support, but he continues to stare into his glass.

MARTIN

We can't afford it! Why bother talking about it?

A long silence follows.

WANDA

I hope Emma likes chicken?

BY THE LETTER

MARTIN
(*Shakes his head*) She doesn't eat animal protein. Nothing with eyes and a mother.

LARRY
(*Laughs out loud*) That's a lot of things. No eyes and a mother.

MARTIN
Chickens have eyes.

LARRY
And mothers.

MARTIN
No chicken for her. She went total vegan last year. She tried to convince me, but I said I didn't want to put any additional burden on you (*points to WANDA*). She thought it was so sweet of me, isn't it?

WANDA
We were supposed to have shrimp cocktail, too.

MARTIN
Nope! Eyes and mothers.

WANDA
Even if their heads are already off? No more eyes.

MARTIN
No way! That's cheating. She's very strict about it.

WANDA
And chocolate mousse?

MARTIN
Afraid not. It's made with animal protein. Besides, she says that miserable peasants harvest the cacao beans under exploitative conditions. You

really have to be so careful these days. Food's not just nourishment, it's a political statement of social solidarity. That's what she says.

> *MARTIN nods. Both WANDA and LARRY take large gulps of their drinks.*

WANDA
We have a salad; would that be all right? With croutons and bits of cheese?

MARTIN
(*Shakes her head*) Animal proteins. She'd have to pick out all the cheese. That would be really hard on her.

> *LARRY stands up and takes out his wallet. He extracts forty dollars and hands them to MARTIN.*

LARRY
Here's forty bucks for you. Go have a nice dinner at that new vegan place downtown. Happy birthday!

> *MARTIN stands up. He hasn't touched his orange juice. MARTIN reaches forward, leaning over the coffee table, and takes the money from LARRY.*

MARTIN
Are you sure? I know how tight money is around here. And Grandpa and Grandma wanted to see me and meet Emma, too.

LARRY
Yes, I'm sure. Your grandparents will be back in an hour or so and we'll just have dinner with them. It will be fine. Happy birthday!

BY THE LETTER

MARTIN

Thanks Dad. (*Pockets the money and steps around the coffee table and hugs LARRY before turning to his WANDA*) Are you sure? I know you went to a lot of trouble to prepare the dinner.

WANDA

Of course, it was no trouble at all. Mom and Dad will be glad to see you and meet Emma another time.

MARTIN

I'll text Emma and tell her to meet me at the vegan restaurant. I'll catch the bus to get downtown. I'm sorry she can't meet you. Maybe next time.

MARTIN leaves. WANDA returns to the couch and sits down next to LARRY.

WANDA

I'm so sorry.

LARRY

Bitch!

WANDA

(*Looks shocked*) Me!

LARRY

No, Emma. I'm so glad she'll be at Columbia and he'll be right here in state somewhere. Out of sight, out of mind. (*Stands up and reaches to WANDA and takes her by the hands*) The table looks beautiful. I'm sure your parents will appreciate the dishes and the meal. (*Looks at his watch*) They should be here shortly. The menu sound's great and I couldn't ask for better company.

WANDA

Really?

LARRY takes her into his arms and gives her a warm hug.

LARRY

Really! (*Holds up his glass*) Can I have another drink while we're waiting? I need one.

WANDA

Sure!

WANDA pours two more drinks and they sit down on the sofa.

LARRY

To our health!

WANDA

And wealth! Let's not forget the money.

LARRY

(*Clicks glasses*) Don't I wish.

BLACKOUT

SCENE III

HALLOWEEN (INSIGHT)

SETTING

    Kevin and Victoria's home. Jacob and Sophia are sitting at the dining room table. Jacob is leafing through documents. Sophia is looking at a book of recipes. There is a bowl of green beans on the table as well.

SOPHIA

This recipe looks good: Marinated beef tips with fresh green beans with hollandaise sauce. I think your parents will really enjoy it.

JACOB

It makes me sick!

SOPHIA

Hollandaise sauce?

JACOB

No, of course not. (*Shoves a paper over to SOPHIA*) Look at this!

SOPHIA

What is it?

JACOB
It's Dad's bank statement.

SOPHIA
So?

JACOB
Look at this. (*Points to the paper*) There's a $3,200 monthly withdrawal.

SOPHIA
What is it?

JACOB
It's a mortgage payment.

SOPHIA
Your parents have owned this home for 50 years. A mortgage on what?

JACOB
Wanda and Larry's home, of course. It makes me physically ill. This has been going on for years.

SOPHIA
How do you even know about this?

JACOB
Because as prospective executor of their estate, I get copies of their financial statements. Supposedly it's to familiarize me with their accounts.

SOPHIA
So, what does it matter if Mom and Dad pay Wanda and Larry's mortgage? They can afford it, can't they?

JACOB stands up and replaces the statement in a binder.

JACOB

Of course they can, but it's the principle. My folks are just enabling! They are keeping Wanda and Larry in a perpetual state of infantilism. It's an outrage! Mom and Dad just won't set limits. Dad won't do the tough love thing. It's a disgrace.

> *SOPHIA sets down the cookbook and reaches for the bowl of green beans. SOPHIA pushes it in JACOB's direction.*

SOPHIA

Here! Help me break off the ends of the green beans.

> *JACOB sits down and takes a bean. JACOB snaps off one end and then the other with aggressive determination.*

SOPHIA

And what about Dylan?

JACOB

What about him?

SOPHIA

We take care of Patricia four times a week.

JACOB

She's our granddaughter. That's completely different.

SOPHIA

Yes, and Wanda and Larry are Dad and Mom's daughter and son-in-law. They're just trying to help them out of a tough economic situation.

JACOB

It's not the same! Patricia's a little girl, not a grown woman. She's not supposed to be independent.

SOPHIA

And Dylan's a grown man, even if he's still our son.

JACOB

Dylan is working hard and has struggled as a single father. He has weird shifts and there just isn't any way he can take care of Patricia without our help. Wanda and Larry are both able-bodied adults and should both be working. Their kids are old enough to take care of themselves and they are just frittering away their time. They've made a series of bad decisions and they're still making them.

SOPHIA

Like Dylan? Like having a child in his teens and not maintaining a single stable relationship for years, besides with us, of course?

JACOB

I still don't think the two situations are comparable.

The doorbell interrupts their conversation. SOPHIA gets up and lets DYLAN in through the kitchen door. DYLAN is dressed in his working clothes, including a baseball cap, which he throws onto the table before kissing SOPHIA's cheek.

DYLAN

Hi Mom. Hi Dad.

SOPHIA

Maybe you can help us get these green beans ready.

DYLAN

Naw! No manual labor for me after work (*pulls up a chair and sits at the table.*) Where's Grandpa and Grandma?

BY THE LETTER

SOPHIA

They'll be here soon. They're just running some errands.

JACOB

What's new with you?

DYLAN

They've changed my shift at work again. Would you mind picking up Patty at school tomorrow and keeping her overnight again?

JACOB

Of course not. (*Looks over at SOPHIA, who gives him an inquisitive look.*)

DYLAN

And she might have some homework, too. She's got a social studies project to do, or something like that.

JACOB

Any specific subject?

DYLAN

Something to do with a state. I think she picked Louisiana. (*Pauses and picks up a green bean, which he twirls around his fingers before plopping back in the bowl*) She only told me yesterday. She's got to get a bunch of pictures about the state: state bird, state flower, state song, and some famous people from there. And she needs to get one of those special display boards, you know, the ones that open out in three sections.

SOPHIA

(*Pauses*) A tri-fold.

DYLAN

Yeah, a tri-fold. You're so smart.

SOPHIA

And when is this project due?

                           DYLAN

Day after tomorrow, of course. (*Pops one of the beans in his mouth and mashes on it a moment before spitting it out in his hand and depositing it onto the table*) Yeah, I know. It's short notice. But my printer's out of ink and then they changed the shifts on me. And Patty didn't tell me about this until this morning, of course. She can be such a little devil some time.

                           SOPHIA

Anything else?

                           DYLAN

Well, it's getting close to Halloween and Patty said she wanted to be a princess. I mean like a real one, with a big gown and a crown and all that. I know you're a terrific seamstress. (*Grabs SOPHIA's hand*) Oh pretty please, can you make her a beautiful princess gown? (*Pauses*) Or maybe Grandma can do it? She'll be here soon, won't she?

                           SOPHIA

Let's leave you Grandma out of this. We're here to make them a meal, not ask them to help Patty. (*Pauses*) You know I'm involved with a big project with the historical society right now (*extracts her hands from his.*) Halloween's only a week away. I'm not sure I could get it done.

                           DYLAN

I know you can do it, Mom! You're so organized. You can do ten things at once. Can you do it for me, just this one time?

                           SOPHIA

(*Turns to JACOB and smiles*) What do you think, dear? Do you think we can help Dylan out by keeping Patricia, and doing the social studies project and making a fancy Halloween costume?

> *JACOB doesn't answer. He snaps the end off another bean.*

BY THE LETTER

SOPHIA
Or would we just be enabling?

DYLAN
Enabling, what does that mean?

SOPHIA
Your father knows. (*Turns to JACOB*) Don't you, dear?

JACOB
(*Looks at DYLAN's expectant face. After a long pause*) It's complicated.

DYLAN
(*Shrugs his shoulders and looks away*) I don't have time for long explanations. Maybe another time. (*Turns back to SOPHIA*) So you'll pick Patty up at school tomorrow?

SOPHIA
Of course, dear.

DYLAN
And you'll help her make the social studies project?

SOPHIA
Of course, dear.

DYLAN
And you'll work on a princess costume for Halloween?

SOPHIA
Of course, dear.

JACOB
I hope you'll at least pitch in and buy the school supplies and the costume materials, won't you? It seems like the least you can do?

DYLAN
Dad, you know how much they pay me? I can't afford luxuries like that. I can hardly pay the rent and buy groceries. (*Stands up and replaces his baseball cap as he heads for the back door*) I'd really like to help, but I had some unexpected bills with my new girlfriend. You know what I mean (*flashes a big smile and winks at JACOB as he walks toward the door.*) Say hi to Grandpa and Grandma for me.

> *JACOB picks up another bean and pinches of the end with the aggressive gesture of a decapitation.*

SOPHIA
Dad just won't set any limits, eh? No tough love, eh? A disgrace, eh? (*Reaches into the bowl and picks out a few more beans, which she plops down in front of JACOB*) Some more green beans? Or are you adverse to manual labor, too?

JACOB
Hell, no! (*Grabs a bean and holds it to his face as he snaps off the end.*) The two situations are just not the same, not at all.

SOPHIA
Really?

JACOB
When are Mom and Dad going to get here?

SOPHIA
Change the subject, eh? (*Pauses*) Your mom said Dad's appointment was a 3:30 so they shouldn't be too much after 5:00. It'll give us plenty of time to fix the dinner. Maybe you need a drink?

JACOB
Too early to start now, even though I think I need one.

BLACKOUT

SCENE IV

COLUMBUS DAY
(UNFAIR ADVANTAGE)

Wanda and Heather are sorting through a pile of clothing on the dining room table that they fold and place in separate stacks. They get up and walk around as they talk.

WANDA

Look at all this stuff. Mom and Dad have lots of things to give away and so do we. Glad they have a big table. My place is way too small for this job.

HEATHER

Mom said she wanted it all to go to the Good Will for poor people. That's nice. There are a lot of immigrants around who need the help and you sure don't need any of this stuff.

WANDA

I don't want it to go to any illegals. They're getting a free education, free healthcare and their kids are getting into college preferentially. It's a shame for the local families.

HEATHER

So, what's it to you?

WANDA
We pay property taxes and they don't.

HEATHER
That's not true! If they own property, then they pay taxes if they're legal or not. And not only property taxes, but they also pay sales taxes and income taxes. Besides, you live in a rental home so you don't pay any property taxes at all. Isn't that true?

WANDA
I'm sure it's included in the rent. (*Pauses*) Most of those people work for cash only. No one knows how much they work or for whom. Or how long? Or for what wages? (*Pauses*) We pay for them one way or another.

HEATHER
And don't Mom and Dad help pay your rent?

WANDA
That's different. We're just going through a rough patch. Besides, it's a loan, not a gift.

HEATHER
Oh, come on, a no interest long-term loan. Sounds like a gift to me.

WANDA
We're talking about undeserving immigrants, not Larry and me.

HEATHER
Okay, let's talk about immigrants. Are they taking your job, too?

WANDA
Well, not exactly since I'm not working full time, at least not for a fixed salary.

BY THE LETTER

HEATHER
Really? I'd like to see how that's working out, no fixed salary, eh? Under the table payments, undeclared and no withholding, perhaps?

WANDA
It's just friend-to-friend payments for services rendered.

HEATHER
(*Laughs*) Sound's like prostitution.

WANDA
You can be so vulgar! Mrs. Karajian pays me week-to-week based on the hours I spend at her home. I help around the house with some cooking and cleaning and gardening. She really appreciates my coming over and helping her out.

HEATHER
Sounds like black market work to me.

WANDA
Of course, it's not! It's just friendship. (*Pauses*) Besides, she's grateful I can help her out and she views my pay as a gratuity of sorts.

HEATHER
Hmm. I guess that's one way to rationalize things. All those people who employ undeclared immigrants as nannies and gardeners say the same thing, don't they? (*Pauses*) Why do you hate and fear immigrants so much?

WANDA
I told you; they're taking school resources, scholarships and jobs. They fill up all the low-income housing that they take away from the deserving local poor.

HEATHER
(*Laughs*) What deserving local poor? The median income's around here is about $100,000. Do you know anyone undeserving poor and anyone poor around here, for that matter? I don't.

WANDA
Well, not personally, but all that low-paid, illegal immigrant workforce drives down labor costs and drives up rents, especially in this area.

HEATHER
(*Laughs*) What job would you want to take away from these undeserving immigrants? Housekeeping? Gardening? Construction? Restaurant worker? Working in the fields picking fruits and vegetables?

WANDA
No! None of them, but someone younger might want those jobs.

HEATHER
Your son, Martin, perhaps?

WANDA
Of course not! He's college educated and speaks English.

HEATHER
Anyone else you know who might want one of those jobs?

WANDA
You twist everything around. You're just like all those other bleeding-heart liberals who raise taxes and give the money away to freeloaders. You're just a sanctuary city do-gooder.

HEATHER
No! I'm just using common sense. Thousands of places around the U.S. are crying out for decent, hardworking people, wherever they come from. Immigrants revitalize cities that are wasting away when native-born citizens leave to move to places like this.

BY THE LETTER

WANDA
We're not wasting away, not here in Pleasant Valley. And we don't need to be flooded with immigrants to revitalize anything. (*Pauses*) Lots of people around here oppose immigration and they're not all bad people either. Most are God-fearing Christians.

HEATHER
And fascists, perhaps?

WANDA
No, of course not! That's insulting.

HEATHER
Or just xenophobes?

WANDA
No! (*Pauses*) Does that mean not liking foreigners?

HEATHER
Yes.

WANDA
Well, no! We have hordes of East Indians, Chinese, Vietnamese and loads of others who've moved in here. They're usually well-educated professionals: doctors, engineers, computer programmers and some upscale restaurant owners.

HEATHER
So, everyone around here is just a rich, well-educated racist?

WANDA
NO! NO! NO! Good decent people live here, and they oppose illegal immigration (*trails off.*)

HEATHER
Can't think of anyone, can you?

> *WANDA and HEATHER continue to sort through the pile of clothing on the table.*

HEATHER (CONT)
What do you really think about the Karajians?

WANDA
What do you mean?

HEATHER
You work with old Mrs. Karajian. You knew her late husband and their kids. You knew their grandparents. They were immigrants.

WANDA
I'm sure the grandparents were legal immigrants. They're a good, decent family. They've been here for decades now.

HEATHER
Yes, a few decades, no more. (*Pauses*) Mrs. Karajian's father and mother both came to American from Armenia as penniless political refugees in the 1920's. Kurds and Turks massacred over a million and a half Armenians, so they were some of the lucky ones who made it out.

WANDA
That's different. We opened our country to people being killed by their own government. The Armenians were victims of Turkish genocide. (*Pauses*) Who's killing the Mexicans? The Hondurans? The Guatemalans? No one!

HEATHER
Poverty, gangs, disease? Do those count?

WANDA
It's not the same.

HEATHER

People are dying just the same. Their own governments can't or won't protect them. They're coming to survive, to make a living, to raise their families in peace, just like the Karajians did.

WANDA

It's still different.

HEATHER

Why? Because Armenians are white? And Mexicans are brown?

WANDA

Don't be ridiculous!

HEATHER

Am I?

WANDA

(*Slams down the clothing she is folding*) Maybe I am racist! Maybe I am xenophobic! Maybe I'm just scared of foreigners. We can barely make it financially as it is. Poor Larry hangs on to his job by a thread and mostly just to keep the health insurance. If Mom and Dad weren't helping us, we'd be homeless. It scares me to death.

HEATHER

(*Puts down the shirt she is folding*) It's okay to be scared. Just don't use it to make other people's lives miserable when they're miserable enough. (*Pauses*) You're a good person. You can help immigrants, legal or not, without endangering your standard of living.

WANDA

How?

HEATHER

There's a family I know across town that needs clothing, dishes, school supplies, anything. There are 20 huge storage bins in your garage filled with stuff you don't need or want anymore. (*Points to the table*) Here's a table full of clothing that Mom and Dad and you and your grown children will never use again.

WANDA
But I might need it some time?

HEATHER
When?

WANDA
In the future, of course.

HEATHER
For what? For whom? When? (*Shows WANDA a picture of a Hispanic girl and boy*) This is Maria. She's ten. And this is Miguel. He's eight. (*Pauses and hands the picture to WANDA*) Their father's still in Mexico. Their mother works as a house keeper. (*Looks around*) I know your place is a bit messy. You might need her help.

WANDA
No way! I'm not going to prison for employing illegal immigrants.

HEATHER
It's not like you're an elected official or something.

WANDA
But it's illegal.

HEATHER
Like you working for Mrs. Karajian?

WANDA
Why would I want to hire someone to do work around my house when I can do that myself?

BY THE LETTER

HEATHER
(*Looks around the room*) Because your place is a mess, at least from what I've seen.

WANDA
That's insulting. (*Pauses*) Well, you do have a point.

HEATHER
Just think about the good you'd be doing for Maria, Miguel and Angelica.

WANDA
Who's Angelica?

HEATHER
The mother.

WANDA
Does she speak English?

HEATHER
More or less. With no more of an accent than Grandpa Karajian had, just a different one. (*Pauses and picks up another shirt*) And you'll get a clean house, you can empty your garage, and you can clean off this table, too, by giving away these clothes to Maria's family.

WANDA
Well, most of these clothes are Mom and Dad's anyway. Mom invited us over to go through them. We do have a lot of stuff at our house, too.

HEATHER
Yeah, I'm not even sure you can see the dining room table in your place. (*Pauses*) Just thinkg, you can make new LatinX friends and enlarge your social circle. What's there not to like about that plan? Social capital building and charity at the same time!

WANDA

You and your weird ideas. "Social capital," sounds like something Karl Marx would say. (*Pauses*) Would the kids come to our house, too?

HEATHER

Of course not! They're in school learning English among other subjects.

WANDA

At the local taxpayer's expense.

HEATHER

(*Reproachfully*) Come on. I thought you'd turned over a new, charitable leaf.

WANDA

I guess immigrant children have to learn, too.

HEATHER

Even the illegal ones, I suppose?

WANDA

Even the illegal ones.

HEATHER

Right! So let's finish this folding these clothes before happy hour. Mom and Dad should be back soon and we'll have everything set to go over to Good Will. Besides, I think we all deserve some happiness at happy hour. Johnny Walker's waiting. Dad's favorite.

> *WANDA and HEATHER stack up the clothing in neat piles. WANDA gets two glasses, fills them and presents HEATHER with a glass. Both raise their glasses and clink them.*

BY THE LETTER

WANDA
Yes, everyone does deserve some happiness. To happiness!

HEATHER
To happiness!

BLACKOUT

ACT II

SCENE I

GOOD FRIDAY (BURYING BARBIE)

HEATHER and DANIEL play themselves but transform into younger versions of themselves when they go into the garden from the dining room. It is a flashback to when they were young adolescents. HEATHER is 16 or so. HEATHER plays this character in an adolescent-like fashion. Dressed in 70's clothing.

DANIEL plays himself as a boy around 14 years old. Dressed in 70's clothing.

The garden is stage left, which is stark and dimly lit. There is a sarcophagus of wood about the size of a fruit crate. It is decorated with various symbols: Egyptian, Mayan, Christian or others. The box is sitting on the stage and is brightly illuminated. There is also a piece of brown cloth that represents dirt. It is used to cover the box at the end of the scene to "bury" it.

BY THE LETTER

HEATHER and DANIEL stand at the window of the dining room and look out into the garden.

HEATHER
Remember this place (*points to the garden*).

DANIEL
How could I forget it? We spent hours out there playing.

HEATHER
Yeah, playing dolls. Remember that?

DANIEL
(*Sighs*) Of course.

HEATHER
Remember the day you buried Barbie?

DANIEL
(*Pauses*) Yes, of course. I remember every word (*Steps out into the garden and puts on a baseball cap. Transforms himself into a 14-year-old boy. Looks back at HEATHER.*) What about you?

HEATHER
Every word. (*Steps out into the garden and pulls on a tie-dyed shirt.*)

DANIEL is holding a Barbie doll, which he is wrapping in strips of cloth. A shovel is sitting on the ground next to him. HEATHER sneaks up from behind and surprises DANIEL.

HEATHER
(*Yelling*) What are you doing?

DANIEL

(*Stops and tries to hide the partially wrapped Barbie doll behind his back*) Nothing!

HEATHER

That's not true. I can see you're doing something. (*Tries to yank the doll away from DANIEL.*)

DANIEL

NO!

DANIEL and HEATHER struggle until HEATHER succeeds in snatching the doll from behind his back.

HEATHER

(*Holds the doll up in triumph*) Got it! (*Partially unwraps the doll*) It's my Barbie.

DANIEL

No, it's not.

HEATHER

Yes it is. (*Unwraps the doll, which is naked*) It's naked! (*Turns to DANIEL*) What were you doing, you little pervert?

DANIEL

Nothing (*tries to hide the sarcophagus.*)

HEATHER

(*Pushes him aside and looks at the box*) It's a coffin.

DANIEL

No! It's a sarcophagus.

BY THE LETTER

HEATHER
(*Looks at the shovel lying nearby*) You were going to bury Barbie, weren't you? You are a little pervert!

DANIEL
(*Quietly*) Yes, I was. But I'm not a pervert.

HEATHER
Yes, you are! You're a fourteen-year-old boy who still plays with dolls with the girls instead of football with the boys. And now this! What on earth are you trying to accomplish?

DANIEL
Nothing! It was just an experiment. I wanted to bury Barbie and then dig her up in a few years and see what happened to her.

HEATHER
(*Laughs*) What do you think is going to happen? She's made out of plastic. She'll be here in a thousand years when all of us are dead and decayed. (*Pauses*) You're ridiculous!

DANIEL
No more ridiculous than you dressing in boy's clothing.

HEATHER
What are you talking about? That's crazy!

DANIEL
I've seen you. Not just in jeans and that sort of thing, but in this, too! (*Reaches in the box and pulls out a jock strap*) What does a sixteen-year-old girl need with a jock strap? Tell me that if you're so smart!

HEATHER
You're lying. You've never seen me put that thing on.

DANIEL
(*Waving the jock strap around*) Oh yes I have! And that's not all. (*Pulls a football jersey out of the box*) What about this thing? A football jersey. (*Pauses*) A week ago when you thought I was asleep, I came downstairs and saw you parading around in your jock strap and your football jersey. That's all. Nothing else. Just those two things. (*Pauses*) Oh yes, and a banana in the jock strap, of course. (*Pulls a plastic banana from the box*) Mustn't forget the crowning touch, the plastic banana.

HEATHER
You're lying, you perverted little creep. (*Knocks the objects out of DANIEL's hands. Lunges at DANIEL and starts to strangle him.*)

DANIEL
(*Choking but still talking*) It's true and you know it.

> *DANIEL struggles with HEATHER and manages to break free. HEATHER chases DANIEL around the box a few times before HEATHER stops and sits down next to the box.*

HEATHER
(*Starts to whimper*) Don't tell anyone, please don't tell anyone. The girls at school would destroy me. It would be all around school in ten minutes.

DANIEL
That long? I'd say more like three.

HEATHER
Please don't tell anyone, I beg you!

DANIEL
Why should I? Unless, of course, you tell anyone about me burying Barbie. The guys at school might find it a bit bizarre. (*Sits down next to HEATHER*) That's okay. I'm not going to tell anyone about you or the

BY THE LETTER

DANIEL
(*Shrugs his shoulders*) Sure, so what?

HEATHER
Have you ever dreamed of him naked? Kissing him?

DANIEL
No! That's sick.

HEATHER
Maybe? But I see how you look at him and he even sometimes looks at you in a strange way. I bet he'd like to play with your little weenie and you would like that a lot, wouldn't you?

DANIEL
(*Stands up*) Stop it! Shut up! You're perverted!

HEATHER
(*Picks up the jock strap and swings it around*) I bet Rob fills this up and when his dick gets all stiff and hard, I bet it jumps right out of the top. (*Hands DANIEL the jock strap*) Here! It's yours. Put it on and rub it against your little weenie and think of Rob.

DANIEL
(*Throws it back into the box*) No! This is wrong. This is sick. You're just talking filth.

HEATHER
(*Confronts DANIEL*) Am I? Tell me I'm lying. Tell me you've never had those thoughts!

DANIEL
I haven't.

HEATHER
Liar! Liar! LIAR!

DANIEL

(*Sits down and speaks quietly*) Yes, I have had those thoughts sometimes.

HEATHER

(*Puts her arm around DANIEL*) It's okay. Everyone does, I think, it's just that some people have stronger thoughts than others. And in some people, they stay around and in others they go away.

DANIEL

(*Pushes HEATHER's arm away*) You don't know what you're talking about. You're no psychiatrist.

HEATHER

No, I'm not.

DANIEL

(*Jumps up*) Let's bury it all: Barbie, the jockstrap, the jersey. We need to bury it all now.

HEATHER

Okay, if you want to.

> *DANIEL takes the shovel and begins to mimic frantically shoveling. HEATHER holds the box and watches DANIEL work.*

HEATHER

It won't help. You can bury everything, but Barbie will take on a life of her own. And all the pushing and shoving and denying will be like trying to hold back the tide. (*Looks at DANIEL*) You can't hold back the tide. Trust me, I've tied. It won't work. I even tried to will my periods to stop so I wouldn't grow up. But it didn't work for me and burying Barbie won't work for you either.

BY THE LETTER

DANIEL
Yes, it will! I can bury Barbie and all those ideas and feelings will die and shrivel up until nothing is left. It's got to work.

HEATHER
(*Calmly*) No, it won't. Barbie and everything she represents in your little mind will kick and scream in your head until she bursts out like the Resurrection of Christ.

DANIEL
That's blasphemy.

HEATHER
No, it's not. It's true. Barbie will twist and turn and grow and grow in your mind. (*Takes the doll and waves it around DANIEL*) She's never going to die and she'll never leave you!

DANIEL
Give her to me! (*Grabs the doll and shoves it into the box and closes the top*) There! She's gone! And all those weird, evil thoughts are gone with her.

HEATHER
I wish you were right, little brother. (*Makes the sign of the cross and begins to pray*) Oh Barbie, blessed are thou among dolls. May your soul rest in peace. May your body wait in anticipation of the Second Coming of Christ when your flesh shall be made incorruptible and you shall rise from the dead! (*Pauses*) And give peace to your faithful servant, Daniel. May his days and nights be spared from the misery of temptation and may his soul know peace from all anxiety. (*Throws an imaginary clot of earth on the box*) In the name of the Father, the Son and the Holy Ghost. (*Makes the sign of the cross again*) Amen.

DANIEL
(*Makes the sign of the cross*) Amen. Rest in peace.

DANIEL covers the box with a piece of brown cloth. Mimics shoveling. Finishes shoveling and shoulders the shovel. Makes the sign of the cross.

HEATHER

(*Laughs loudly*) Let me know when you're ready to let Barbie out. I'll talk to you then, little brother. (*Pauses*) By the way, I wouldn't share any of this with Mom and Dad if I were you.

DANIEL

Hell no! They'd never be able to handle any of this.

HEATHER

Not now, but maybe someday. They might be more open-minded than you think.

DANIEL

(*Shakes his head*) No, never! It would kill them both.

HEATHER

Never say never! It would only kill the dreams and illusions they have for us.

DANIEL

That's bad enough, isn't it? (*Pauses*) They'd kick us both out of the house and disown us.

HEATHER

Maybe and maybe not. Besides I'll be long gone by then, free and independent and they won't be able to do a thing except to either accept me for what I am or cut me off entirely. They've got to learn to be flexible, to bend with the wind and the changing times.

DANIEL

Sounds pretty unlikely. They might break before they come to that sort of acceptance.

HEATHER

Time will tell. People are a lot more flexible than you think, even Mom and Dad. I suspect they've experienced more than we suspect. (*Gives DANIEL her hand*) Here, take my hand. Let me lead you out of the valley of death and away from temptation.

DANIEL

Thanks.

> *HEATHER takes DANIEL's free hand and leads him back into the dining room. They revert to their adult selves.*

DANIEL

That was an intense trip down memory lane.

HEATHER

Yes, it was. Although it seemed like it just happened. (*Pauses*) It's funny how some things stick with you and others disappear with time.

DANIEL

Yes. (*Pauses*) The past is prologue. And the child is father to the man. It's hard to tell what's really important when it's happening. Only later can we separate the wheat from the chaff.

HEATHER

You've become quite the philosopher.

DANIEL

Does that bother you?

HEATHER

Not me, but it certainly bothers Jacob.

DANIEL

Yeah, that's an understatement.

HEATHER

I'm not sure I'm on his favorite list either.

DANIEL

That's true, but it's not like his feelings toward me. There's something visceral about it. It's not an intellectual thing, it's a gut thing.

HEATHER

It's hard to argue with the visceral, isn't it?

DANIEL

Impossible. It's neuro-anatomical. It's a limbic response, not a cortical one.

HEATHER

Philosophical and neuro-anatomical. Good grief. Can you just talk like a normal person?

DANIEL

No, I can't. I don't think either of us are that "normal." And that's part of the problem, isn't it? For us and for our dear brother, Jacob?

HEATHER

You're right. But I say "vive la difference." Jacob will have his own demons to deal with in time, little brother. (*gives DANIEL a hug and leads him off stage.*)

BLACKOUT

SCENE II

FATHER'S DAY (ONLY OUR DNA)

A large table with a big cooking pot sits in the garden portion of the stage. There are two chairs. Jacob and Daniel are cutting up things to put in the large gumbo pot. Jacob has the vegetables and Daniel has the meat. They both have knives (not real ones because they fight with them.) There are a couple of large wooden spoons for stirring.

DANIEL
No! We can't leave Wanda out of the party preparations.

JACOB
Why not?

DANIEL
Because she's part of the family. She's our sister, for heaven's sake. And this party's for Dad from his children, all of them.

JACOB
Well, if she were really part of the family then she would contribute to it.

DANIEL
Everyone contributes what they can. Wanda just doesn't have the same resources.

JACOB
Not the same resources! She's squandered everything she's ever gotten by making stupid decisions. Asking her to pitch in anything to this party is useless. Besides, it would be awkward for her. She would feel bad that we were buying all the supplies and she buys nothing. That's awkward.

DANIEL
Isn't it more awkward leaving her out entirely?

JACOB
We're not leaving her out. When the gumbo's done and the party's ready, she can come and eat with us like all the other guests.

DANIEL
But that's the point. It's a party for Dad and he's father to all of us, not just you and me. She's our sister, not just another guest.

JACOB
She can't bring anything! She doesn't have anything to offer. Don't you get it? She just lives off Dad and Mom's charity and they squanders that, too. She's worse than a guest; she's a blood-sucking parasite!

DANIEL
She could cut up vegetables and meat. She could stir the pot. She could set the table. There's a lot Wanda could contribute without buying anything.

JACOB
Don't be a fool. She has so many problems; she doesn't have the time, the money, or the inclination to add anything to this party, not even her cheerful disposition.

BY THE LETTER

DANIEL
Why don't you let her decide?

JACOB
(*Turns toward DANIEL in anger.*) Do you really want to sabotage this event? We can do this just fine together, just the two of us. In fact, I could do it myself if I wanted to, and you know it as well as I do. Why transform this event into a three-ring circus by including our dear loser sister?

DANIEL
Because the preparations are just as important as the final product. We're the ones who are squandering an opportunity to create some sibling memories, some social bonding.

JACOB:
For God's sake, stop it with the liberal touchie-feely crap!

DANIEL
It's not crap! (*Stands up and walks around*) Bringing people together is essentially moral. Tearing them apart, or keeping them apart (*points his knife at JACOB*) is immoral. (*Pauses*) We have an opportunity to create some bonding time together. In fact, it's important because we would be joining together people who don't think alike.

JACOB
(*Interrupting DANIEL*) That's the truth! Or act alike for that matter. For better or worse, you and I have virtually nothing in common, never have, and never will. Our interests, politics, hobbies, talents, values, views on life, couldn't be more different. And to that, I say, so be it. *Vive la difference*! We're not buddies, never have been, never will be. To that, I also say, so be it! While we're brothers, we're not close, never have been, never will be. That's just the way it is, and I for one am okay with that.

DANIEL
But that's what's so important. If we thought alike, then coming together would just be like bringing together people who belong to the same

church or the Klu Klux Klan for that matter. That's not as important or as significant as bringing together people who really don't even like each other, especially siblings.

JACOB

You sound just like Heather with all her social capital crap. It's incredible how much you two talk alike.

DANIEL

She's right sometimes. She organizes for several groups and reads a lot. Social capital comes from Robert Putnam's book, "Bowling Alone in America." You might like it.

JACOB

(*Throws down his knife and stands up*) Would you please spare me your pontification? I get your point. (*Pauses*) I can already see it. This is supposed to be Dad's party and you somehow manage to monopolize all the attention by giving a speech about the importance of the family and social capital building. Yes, it's interesting. Yes, it's important. But this party is not about you. It's about Dad. (*Swings his arms around*) And what's more, when I talk to Dad, he's always talking about you. "Daniel this, Daniel, that." Don't you think I get tired of hearing all that shit all the time? It makes me sick to my stomach!

DANIEL

You're jealous, aren't you?

JACOB

No! I'm disgusted. What do you think it feels like just sitting there and listening to Dad extol your virtues, your accomplishments, your talents, and your contributions to the world? (*Pauses.*) And the thought of you prancing around deciding what's "fun" for everyone else to do or even what and when to eat, yelling "*A table! A table!*" in French to everyone, it revolts me. Your need to continually be the center of attention is legendary. Even your belief that it would be "fun" for everyone to be here at the same time is presumptuous. Says who? Says you! And I guess that's enough in your "humble" opinion. (*Yells*) It's boring! It's frustrating! It's painful!

DANIEL

(*Walks over to JACOB*) We both have the same father. We both have the same needs. We share the same upbringing. We're really both very much alike (*reaches out to touch JACOB.*)

JACOB

(*Pulls away*) No! Don't touch me! All your fake expressions of affection, they're artificial crap. (*Pauses*) We're not alike! We don't share anything but our genes, our DNA!

DANIEL

(*Shrugs and moves away*) Nothing but our genes, eh? That's a lot already. Add to that our similar childhood experiences and we share both nature and nurture. That's an awful lot to share, in my humble opinion.

JACOB

(*Advances toward his brother*) Humble! Humble! There's not a humble bone in your body and you know it. You take over everything. You're like some sort of black hole that attracts all the energy. You suck in the light so that there is nothing else left; no warmth, no oxygen, and no life expect yours. (*Pauses*) Over the years, I've attempted on many occasions to figure out what it is about you that most sticks in my craw. Each time, I come to the same conclusion. It's your long-standing and oft-displayed arrogance and pomposity. Your narcissism is simply breathtaking. It truly is all about you. Your education and knowledge are second to none. Your opinions are omnipotent. Your pronouncements are all brilliant. Your ideas are all wonderful. Your company is the envy of all lesser people. And, as the old line goes, if you don't think so, just ask. I'm not sure what I have to do to make it clearer to you that I don't share your opinions about yourself. Just because something is your idea doesn't necessarily make it brilliant. I, for one, do not believe that all your ideas are veritable pearls dropping off the end of your tongue. You put your pants on one leg at a time, just like us mere mortals.

DANIEL
(*Speaks in a very soothing voice*) I sense anger. I sense frustration. Don't you think it's good we're having a cathartic conversation?

JACOB
Cathartic! (*Returns and grabs the knife, pointing it in DANIEL's direction*) You know what would be cathartic?

DANIEL
Don't tell me? You want to kill me. You think that if I were out of the way that everything would be perfect. You think you would finally be Daddy's favorite because I'd be gone. That's what you're thinking, isn't it?

JACOB
(*Continues to advance*) Those thoughts have crossed my mind. I am entitled to my opinions and will express them when and where I choose.

DANIEL
(*Grabs a large wooden spoon and goes into fencing position*) Yes, killing me would certainly solve a lot of your problems. Or so you think. *En garde*!

> JACOB *advances and they have a choreographed combat, like a fencing match. As they fight,* DANIEL *continues to talk.*

DANIEL
You kill me and you'd go to prison. You'd break Mom and Dad's hearts. You'd go to the electric chair and cause incredible pain to your family. (*Continues to fight*) And then, your sisters that you despise so much would be the only ones left to inherit all of Dad's wealth. She would be dancing on both of our graves. Did you think about that?

JACOB
(*Steps away and lowers his knife*) *Touché*!

BY THE LETTER

JACOB and DANIEL return to the table and resume cutting vegetables and meat and putting it into the gumbo pot. There is a long silence.

DANIEL

(*Looks into the pot*) It smells good.

JACOB

You always win, don't you? One way or another, you always win.

DANIEL

It's not a contest. Dad loves all of us the same way.

JACOB

(*Sarcastically*) Right.

DANIEL

(*Laughs and then pauses*) He just loves some of us more than others. (*Leans toward JACOB*) You know what Dad calls me sometimes?

JACOB

No.

DANIEL

"His favorite son."

JACOB

You're lying!

DANIEL

No I'm not. As God is my witness!

JACOB

I don't believe you. Besides, why are you telling me this?

DANIEL
Because it's the truth, and the truth shall set us free.

JACOB
I don't believe you.

DANIEL
(*Stands up, drops his knife and crosses his heart*) Cross my heart and hope to die (*looks heavenward*).

> *JACOB jumps up and stabs DANIEL in the heart. DANIEL, with a surprised look on his face, falls to the ground. JACOB looks at DANIEL and goes back to his chair, where he sits down. JACOB pulls out a cell phone and dials.*

JACOB
Hello, 911? There's been an accident. (*Pauses.*) Yes, someone's badly hurt. (*Pauses*) He slipped and fell on a knife. (*Pauses.*) Yes, we're at 1812 Sava Street. I'll be here waiting for you. (*Dials again*) Dylan, this is Dad. (*Pauses*) I have a delicate situation here. Can you send one of your most trusted detectives this way for the investigation? (*Pauses*) Yes, there's been a bad accident with your Uncle Daniel here at your grandparent's house. (*Pauses*) Yeah, he fell on his own knife. You know how that happens sometimes. And call your grandparents and tell them not to come back to the house now. Tell them to wait and come in a few hours (*Pauses*) Yeah, I know they thought there was going to be a surprise party, but I don't want them here with the police and the ambulance. (*Pauses*) I'll count on you. Thanks. See you soon.

> *JACOB closes the phone and sits down. He takes DANIEL's knife and carefully wipes off the fingerprints and puts it in DANIEL's outstretched hands. JACOB takes his own knife*

and continues to cut up vegetables, which he drops in the gumbo pot. Sirens sound in the distance.

BLACKOUT

ACT III

SCENE I

DAY OF THE DEAD (PEACEFUL REPOSE)

This is a wake. Seven chairs are placed in a semi-circle upstage in the living around a table with a prominent picture of Kevin, draped in black ribbon. There is a single vase with some flowers. Victoria weeps quietly. Wanda wipes her eyes from time to time, as does Sophia. From right to left, the chairs are for Wanda, Larry, Martin, Victoria, Dylan, Sophia and Jacob.

WANDA and JACOB advance toward either other from either side of the table with the picture and meet downstage center

JACOB
(*To WANDA*) You have a lot of nerve, weeping like a Madeleine, your heart breaking from grief. We already saw this with Daniel. That was a real tear-jerking production.

BY THE LETTER

WANDA
What is that supposed to mean? They're both dead and you don't seem very upset this time or with Daniel. (*Wipes her eyes*) Do you think this is really the best place to talk like this?

JACOB
Why not? It's not like Dad's going to hear you or anything. He's dead. Daniel's certainly not listening. He's long gone.

WANDA
I have a right to grieve, don't I?

JACOB
Maybe. But you should feel guilty as hell, not grief-stricken.

WANDA
I'm not guilty at all. Larry and I have always done what we could do for Dad.

JACOB
Done what you can do? That's a joke. You certainly did what you could do all right: sponging off Dad to the bitter end, making them worry about you for years instead of enjoying the last years of his life, poisoning their time with your financial problems. It's a disgrace. If you cry, it's for yourself, not for him.

WANDA
You're hateful and mean and spiteful! Didn't you learn anything from Dad? He was kind and thoughtful and smart and generous. You didn't learn anything, did you?

JACOB
Sure, I did. I learned that you should raise independent children who can solve their own problems and take care of themselves.

WANDA
Yeah! Like Dylan and his love child, the one you're raising like your own. Now that's really independence, isn't it?

JACOB
That's what parents are for.

WANDA
Precisely! And that's just what Dad did and that's just what you reproached him for doing, you hypocrite! At least I'm here, Heather couldn't even bother to make it.

JACOB
That's not true. She's stuck in Florida. It's not her fault if there's a hurricane. Besides, she's always tried her best, which is more than I can say for you.

SOPHIA gets up from her chair and comes over to stand beside JACOB.

SOPHIA
What in the world are you two doing?

WANDA
Please don't get involved. This is between siblings, blood relatives, not in-laws.

SOPHIA
So, I'm not part of the family because I just married into it, is that it?

WANDA
Correct, you're only an in-law and not a blood relative. This is between Jacob and me.

BY THE LETTER

SOPHIA
Being a member of a family is more than blood. It's a question of attitude and responsibility.

WANDA
And I'm not responsible?

SOPHIA
No! Unfortunately, you're not.

WANDA
And your son, he's responsible I guess?

SOPHIA
What's that supposed to mean?

WANDA
How responsible is someone who has a child that he can't raise and leaves it to his parents to take care of?

SOPHIA
Well, at least he's on his own. That's more than I can say for you and Larry. You two have been sucking the lifeblood out of poor Dad and Mom for years.

LARRY steps forward and joins the conversation.

LARRY
What's happening here? You're fighting like cats and dogs at a funeral.

WANDA
Cats and dogs, no! We're being treated as parasites again, sucking the lifeblood from Dad and Mom until there was nothing left to suck. And if you don't believe me, just ask either one of the can-do-no-wrong couple here.

LARRY
For heaven's sake! Is this really the time and place for this discussion? Your Dad isn't even in the ground yet.

WANDA
What better time? Dad's not even cold and we're at each other's throats. Maybe we won't be seeing one another too often after this.

SOPHIA
And that just might be the best thing, too. Jacob can just keep sending you the checks and you can be quiet and leave us alone. You'll get your full inheritance eventually and that should make everything all right.

WANDA
Everything right? Dad's dead, Mom's having a nervous breakdown and doesn't want to live anymore. Her health's going downhill. What's right about all that?

LARRY
(*Pulls at WANDA*) Would you just come and sit down. We don't need to draw any attention to ourselves. It's a funeral, for God's sake, not a group therapy session.

JACOB
Maybe it's both. (*To WANDA and LARRY*) You've been monopolizing Dad and Mom's conversations for years. Maybe now we can strike a new equilibrium.

LARRY
As executor of Dad's estate, I suppose you can do whatever you please. You can cut us off and have us thrown out into the street. Is that what you plan?

JACOB
No, of course not. I'll do what Dad wanted me to do. That's a bit different, wouldn't you agree?

BY THE LETTER

LARRY
(*Pulling at WANDA*) Come on. Let's sit down and think about this.

WANDA
Think about what? The essential goodness of man as epitomized by my brother, the executor, or should I say the executioner? I never thought Daniel's death was an accident. Maybe I worried Dad to death, but I didn't kill him. At least not on purpose.

JACOB
Shut up, stupid cow! Daniel's death was an accident and everyone knows it.

> *DYLAN, JACOB and SOPHIA now come and joins the conversation.*

DYLAN
Mom, is there something wrong?

SOPHIA
No, please just go sit down.

DYLAN
You look upset.

SOPHIA
It's nothing.

WANDA
Yes, go sit down. You can be the dutiful son and obey your parents. It's never too late, you know.

DYLAN
What's that supposed to mean?

WANDA

You know. You enforce the law, but you have trouble keeping a steady girlfriend. I guess you can be faithful to your parents while imposing the responsibility of child rearing on them.

DYLAN

(*To WANDA*) That's nuts. (*To JACOB and SOPHIA*) Is she completely crazy?

WANDA

Nuts! Who's treating who as nuts? And since when has a cop become an expert in psychiatry? If you want to be a psychiatrist, why didn't you just go to college and really make yourself into something.

SOPHIA

What are you talking about? You're the one who never went to college. Dylan finished the academy and he'll get a degree one of these days. You'll see! And you'll still be playing house and living above your means.

VICTORIA sits in her chair and quietly sobs.

MARTIN

(*To WANDA*) Mom, what are you yelling about?

WANDA

We're just discussing your cousin Dylan and his academic achievements.

MARTIN

Come on. He's got a good job and a cute daughter. And we're at Grandpa's funeral for God's sake. Can't you show some respect for the dead?

DYLAN

Thank you, Martin! I appreciate your confidence and I do admire your academic success. I hear you got a full scholarship. That's really cool.

BY THE LETTER

JACOB

(*To MARTIN*) Too bad it's not enough to support your whole family.

LARRY

What's that supposed to mean?

JACOB

I mean that you've been unemployed for years and maybe your son can give you some of his scholarship money to live on.

WANDA

That's a cheap shot! Larry's looked everywhere for a job. I mean everywhere. He's not a spring chicken and we're in the middle of a recession.

JACOB

(*Skeptically*) Right.

LARRY

It's a tough job market now. I followed up on just about every lead. I'm not that young anymore and the recession wiped out the job market. Do you think I really want to collect unemployment?

JACOB

I saw a help wanted sign down at the Burger King. They need workers.

WANDA

(*Raises her voice*) You don't expect someone with a degree in economics to be flipping burgers in some Burger King like a pimply-faced high school student!

LARRY

(*To WANDA*) For God's sake, you'll wake the dead.

WANDA

(*Glances over at the photograph*) Fat chance.

VICTORIA

(*Stands up and moves over to join the circle*) Please stop it! Your Dad and I wanted you to love one another. That's all we really wanted, for you to be happy with your own lives and supportive of your siblings. Love. That's all. Just love.

JACOB

We tolerate one other.

WANDA

Barely.

VICTORIA

(*Goes over and addresses the photo*) Why did you abandon me? Why did you leave me in the middle of all this hatred and bickering? Why couldn't we have died together at the same moment? Why can't I just die right here, right now!

> *JACOB and SOPHIA go over and put their arms around VICTORIA's shoulders.*

JACOB

Come on, Mom. Please don't get upset. I'm here to help you.

WANDA

(*To JACOB and SOPHIA*) And we're not here to help?

SOPHIA

Help do what? You're penniless, over-extended, scatter-brained and unable to run your own household, much less someone else's.

WANDA

(*Lunges at SOPHIA*) You pretentious witch!

> *WANDA and SOPHIA scuffle while JACOB and LARRY try to pull them apart. In the*

confusion, the vase and the picture fall off the table. Everyone steps back in horror.

ALL

Dad!

JACOB

(*To WANDA*) Now look what you've done!

WANDA

Me! (*Starts pounding on JACOB*) It's your fault, you asshole! You're the one who's wrecked everything.

JACOB

Shut up!

LARRY

Don't tell my wife to shut up!

JACOB

I'll tell her to shut up when she crosses the line.

LARRY

What line?

JACOB

The line of decency.

LARRY

So now we're not just parasites, but indecent ones at that. Should we just go away and die to make your life easier?

SOPHIA

It's a thought.

DYLAN

Have you considered Arkansas?

LARRY and WANDA

Arkansas?

MARTIN

Can I just finish college first, please? I don't want to go to school in Arkansas.

> *VICTORIA has gone to the floor and picks up the picture and the scattered flowers.*

VICTORIA

What about Dad? Please help me put this back.

> *The others stop and stare down at VICTORIA and the table and flowers. They all go and help VICTORIA re-arrange the table and readjust the flowers. VICTORIA replaces the photo in the middle.*

VICTORIA

Can't we all just get along?

ALL

What?

VICTORIA

I said, can't we all just get along?

> *The all look and one another and then go back to their seats and sit down. Lights dim to dark as "All We Need is Love" plays.)*

BLACKOUT

SCENE II

CHRISTMAS (MAKING WEATHS)

Sophia and Wanda are working at the dining room table making Christmas wreaths. They tie on red ribbons. They may be seated or standing behind the table. There are a couple of boxes with partially completed and finished wreaths.

SOPHIA
(*Holds up a wreath*) How does this one look?

WANDA
Fine.

SOPHIA
Don't you think the bow's a bit too large?

WANDA
No, it looks fine.

SOPHIA
Is it crooked? I think it's a little too much to the right.

WANDA

No, Sophia! It's not too big, not too small and not crooked. It's perfect. (*Pauses*) For heaven's sake, what does it matter? It's for dead people anyway.

SOPHIA

(*Slams down her wreath*) Wanda! These are for deceased veterans, including your Mom and Dad, and we owe them the respect they earned through their service to our country. I'm glad you're here and that we're working together, but don't be disrespectful! Especially here in their home!

WANDA

Sorry! I came over to help, not to make problems. I thought this might give us a fresh start in our relationship. Maybe we can learn to get along in the spirit of the season. I've tried to put our past confrontations behind me, especially the fiasco at Dad's funeral.

SOPHIA

Yes, that was quite a scene. Maybe we can let bygones be bygones. Either way, I appreciate your thoughtfulness in wanting to help. I really do. It's for a wonderful cause.

> *WANDA and SOPHIA work in silence for a few seconds.*

SOPHIA

Did you hear about Victoria's mother's ashes?

WANDA

Victoria, you mean Mom?

SOPHIA

Yes, of course. How many Victoria's do you know?

WANDA

I usually call her Mom, not Victoria. So, what happened?

BY THE LETTER

SOPHIA
Well, Victoria had her mother cremated decades ago and then her ashes got lost somewhere in the columbarium.

WANDA
Really?

SOPHIA
Yes, really! And when one of Victoria's surviving sisters wanted to know what happened to the ashes, she called Dylan because she knew he was a detective. He finally tracked down the funeral urn. (*Pauses*) It was stuck up on a shelf in the back of a building with a bunch of other urns and a sign marked "Pending final disposition."

WANDA
(*Laughs*) That's pretty funny. Pending final disposition, eh?

SOPHIA
(*Serious*) What's funny about that?

WANDA
There's nothing more final than death, followed by cremation. Except of course if you're one of those people who have their ashes made into a ceramic Raku vase by a potter.

SOPHIA
That can't be true.

WANDA
Yes, it is, I swear to God. And when I die, Larry can turn me into a big pot and stuff flowers into me from time to time.

SOPHIA
You can be so ridiculous.

WANDA

No, it's a nice idea. There's nothing ridiculous about perpetuating beauty. (*Works on her wreath*) What'll I care, anyway?

SOPHIA

You may not care, but I will. The dead need to be honored and remembered, just like Kevin and Victoria. I'll make sure you're in a registry somewhere so that Martin will know exactly which pot you're in and where it ends up. I swear to God I will!

WANDA

No need to swear. I believe you. Martin, however, will never be bothered by such details. (*Holds up her completed wreath*) How does this one look?

SOPHIA

If that's the best you can do, I guess it's okay.

WANDA

(*Takes another wreath to tie on a bow*) Did you hear about Charlie?

SOPHIA

My nephew, Charlie? No, what about him?

WANDA

He lost his apartment, his car, his job, his wife and their son, all within a year.

SOPHIA

What happened this time?

WANDA

Drugs again.

SOPHIA

Which drug this time?

BY THE LETTER

WANDA
I don't know. Someone said it was "Krocodil" or something nasty like that. Some variation of heroin, mixed with fentanyl. (*Works on her wreath*) He's been in and out of rehab for the last few years. Now's he's in some sleazy halfway house.

SOPHIA
I try not to follow him too closely now. I know he's a relative, but he's a loser. He was loser as a kid and he's a loser now as an adult.

WANDA
He's a veteran, too, you know. I thought veterans needed and deserved our respect.

SOPHIA
Yes, I know he was a veteran, who got dishonorably discharged for drug use!

WANDA
So, he doesn't get a wreath, or even a site in the military cemetery when he dies?

SOPHIA
Of course not, you know that. Shooting yourself up with God knows what and frying your brain is not the same thing as dying in the service of your country.

WANDA
I heard he had PTSD and that made him start drugs. He also lost his left arm from shooting up. It went into an artery and his arm just sort of sloughed off. At least that's what I heard. They said his whole arm turned black and horrible and they just had to chop it off above the elbow. That's before his wife finally left him with their son. Not because of the arm, but because she just couldn't take it anymore.

SOPHIA

Horrible. It's all too horrible!

WANDA

(*Works on her wreath. Completes the bow and shows it to SOPHIA*) Can we put aside a wreath for Charlie's halfway house?

SOPHIA

Of course not! These are for deserving veterans only.

WANDA

Come on, Sophia, one wreath won't make any difference. Charlie's just about dead anyway.

SOPHIA

Certainly not!

WANDA

That halfway house of his probably needs a little Christmas cheer.

SOPHIA

Stop! (*Puts down her wreath*) Good God-fearing, patriotic people donated money to honor our deceased veterans with Christmas wreaths. Doing anything else with them would be sacrilegious.

WANDA

But some living people need them more than the dead, don't you think?

SOPHIA

The dead are the deserving ones here, not the undeserving living.

WANDA

(*Reaches out and touches SOPHIA.*) Sophia, Charlie's your nephew, not mine. We knew him because he went to school with Martin, that's all. He needs some compassion, too. He might get a tiny shred of pleasure from a Christmas wreath from both of us on his door. Can we re-focus our energy here a little bit on the living?

SOPHIA

NO!

WANDA

(*Takes a twenty-dollar bill from her pocket*) Here's a twenty. I'll buy a wreath from you for Charlie. You can replace it.

SOPHIA

No! It's dishonest. Besides, you and Larry don't have any extra money to spare. You couldn't even pay the rent without your parent's money.

WANDA

Please don't go there. We're making a fresh start, remember? Let's bury the dead and move on. Let me decide what I can spend on what. (*Sets the money on the table and continues to work on a wreath*) You know what Jesus said?

SOPHIA

Don't take the Lord's name in vain!

WANDA

I'm not!

SOPHIA

Is this some sort of perverse joke?

WANDA

No, I swear.

SOPHIA

(*Reconsiders*) Okay, what did Jesus say?

WANDA

(*Sets down her wreath*) He told his disciples "follow me and let the dead bury the dead."

SOPHIA

Jesus said that? (*Pauses*) He said so many things.

WANDA

Yes, he did.

SOPHIA

What do you think that means anyway?

WANDA

I'm no religious expert, but I think it means that the people who are spiritually dead are the ones that focus on those who are already physically dead. I think it's a metaphor.

SOPHIA

A metaphor, eh? I didn't realize you were so intellectual.

WANDA

Yeah, you just thought I was dumb and superficial because I didn't finish college. I've heard you say so to Jacob and to Mom and Dad when they were living. Everyone else went to college except me, of course. Charlie never even tried, at least that's what Martin told us.

SOPHIA

(*Works on the wreath*) I'm sorry. I can be pretty thoughtless sometimes.

WANDA

That's okay. I can be pretty stupid sometimes, too.

SOPHIA

(*Works in silence a few minutes*) Have I become so hard-hearted? So spiritually misdirected?

BY THE LETTER

WANDA

(*Pauses*) Yes, pretty much.

SOPHIA

(*Looks around and sighs*) I guess we can make a replacement wreath. (*Takes the money and hands it and a wreath to WANDA*) Take the money back and take this wreath. Take it over to Charlie's halfway house. If anyone asks you, just say it comes from some veteran's organization.

WANDA

No, I'll tell them it's from both of us, you and me.

SOPHIA

No, please don't. I've turned Charlie away time after time. It was just too hard with him. He's an emotional and economic black hole that sucks everything into it. He'll probably sell the wreath and get some dope.

WANDA

Maybe. (*Takes the wreaths*) And maybe he'll realize it was a gift from generous relatives who still care about him even though he's squandered his life on drugs.

SOPHIA

Don't tell him it's from me. It would break his heart if he knew. I've told him to his face that he was a stupid good-for-nothing, in front of his own child. (*Pauses*) It's too much to think about. (*Returns to making a wreath*) At least the dead leave me in peace. Maybe that's why I'm so comfortable with them.

WANDA

Yes, but living people need us, not the dead.

SOPHIA

Leave now before I change my mind. And don't tell him, please. It needs to be a gift from you and an anonymous donor.

WANDA

(*Leaving*) I'll be back in a couple of hours to help you take the other wreaths to the veteran's cemetery. Mom and Dad won't know the difference, it's not like they're in a hurry, but it's nice that we're working together, some quality time, some social capital building.

SOPHIA

Sounds like some rubbish from Heather.

WANDA

Yes, but she's sometimes right, you know. (*Pauses*) Wait until I get back so I can help you. There are way too many wreaths for you to take out to the cemetery and distribute alone.

SOPHIA

(*Smiles*) Drive carefully and don't hurry. I think the dead can wait for their wreaths a little longer. They won't care and I shouldn't either, should I?

> *WANDA nods and exits and SOPHIA continues to work on a wreath.*

SOPHIA (CONT)

(*Shakes her head*) Let the dead bury the dead.

BLACKOUT

SCENE III

NEW YEAR'S DAY
(THE HOUSE ON SAVA STREET)

Jacob, Heather and Wanda are in Kevin and Victoria's home on Sava Street. There are a few boxes scattered around and some paintings stacked against the wall. There are chairs and a couch in the den and chairs and a table covered with various articles in the living room. The characters get up and move around often. There are two folding chairs off to the side downstage for Kevin and Victoria. They watch and inject comments but the siblings cannot see or hear them. When Kevin and Victoria speak to one another, the action freezes for the others. Their dialogue is separated by ***.

JACOB
NO! I'm not going to run a damn time-share for the convenience of my siblings.

HEATHER
We're not asking for that. We're just asking for the use of the place for a week a year, non-cumulative and non-transferable.

WANDA
We can continue to enjoy Mom and Dad's place and you would get a big tax break in exchange.

JACOB
What do you know about tax breaks?

WANDA
A lot! Larry used to be in real estate, for God's sake.

JACOB
Leave God out of this!

WANDA
If we sign a release of ownership, you can still buy out our portion of the house and get a $100,000 tax reduction over the next ten years. It would be a parent-to-child transfer if authorized by the siblings. What's not to like about that?

HEATHER
We both get a week a year at a date agreeable to you and you have this place to yourselves the other fifty weeks of the year. That's a great deal.

JACOB
No, it's not. I keep the place up, pay the heating and electrical bills, the insurance and the cost of gardening and you two, and your families, waltz in for nothing.

HEATHER and WANDA
Nothing?

HEATHER
We sign away our legal rights, you get the house and significant tax breaks and we get a couple of weeks a year to enjoy the mountains and remember the good times we had here with Mom and Dad.

BY THE LETTER

***

VICTORIA
We did have good times here, didn't we?

KEVIN
Of course! Lots of fun with the family and neighbors. Water skiing and hiking and barbecues, yes, it was all a lot of fun.

VICTORIA
Why do you think they could never get along? Did we cause it?

KEVIN
No! They're grown adults with their own issues and we can't be held responsible. Besides, we're dead.

VICTORIA
True. (*Pauses*) Don't you think Jacob is being unreasonable? It sounds like a good faith offer to me.

KEVIN
It doesn't really matter what we think, does it?

VICTORIA
No, I guess it doesn't. (*Looks around*) The place looks pretty shabby, with all the boxes on the floor and the paintings stacked up against the walls. Daniel always did a lot of the paintings. He was always so very talented. (*Points to one*) I painted that one way back when we bought the place. Not bad at all, if I do say so myself.

KEVIN:
(*To VICTORIA*) You're really very talented, too, both you and Daniel.

VICTORIA

We were talented. (*Pauses*) Now it looks like no one even wants to keep the art, the art that Daniel and I made. That's kind of sad, don't you think?

KENNTH

Yes, very sad. But let's see what happens.

VICTORIA

And your ship model, that doesn't need to end up in a garage sale, does it?

KEVIN

I hope not. (*Pauses*) It would be awful to have it sold for a few dollars and go to someone who doesn't even know who you and I were.

VICTORIA

Maybe some of the love you put into the project will seep through to the viewer. Maybe someone will catch the vibes of the devotion that went into making it. Maybe it'll find a place of honor in someone else's home.

KEVIN

Someone besides our own flesh and blood. (*Pauses*) Maybe you're right. (*Looks over at the siblings*) Let's listen.

***

WANDA

Are a couple of weeks a year that much of a problem? Don't you want to see this place stay in the family?

JACOB

No! I don't want you two going through our things and passing judgment on our interior decorating, our choice of rugs and curtains, our dishes and our linens. Besides, you'd mess everything up.

BY THE LETTER

WANDA
No way! We'd leave the place cleaner and neater than we found it.

JACOB
(*To WANDA*) You've got to be kidding. I don't believe that for a second. I've seen the chaos you live in. If it wasn't for that illegal immigrant maid of yours, it would be an unlivable pigsty.

HEATHER
That's enough! Don't stoop to insults because you've run out of good arguments. (*Pauses*) What's the real problem here? Is it just a control issue? Privacy issue? A personality incompatibility problem? (*Pauses*) What's the real deal?

JACOB
Now you're playing the amateur psychologist, delving into my sinister subconscious to unravel my deep-seated motives.

HEATHER
So, what are they?

WANDA
Yeah, what's the big deal here? I've looked into my hidden motives, maybe you should, too.

JACOB
It doesn't matter. I'm not going to share the old home place with anyone, not even for a minute. I don't want to keep the home place at all. It's not my home place, never has been and never will be. I want a clean break with the past. I want a new beginning in a new year.

HEATHER
And that past includes us as well?

JACOB
Yes!

WANDA

And Mom and Dad, too? Are you breaking with them, too? Were they so bad to deserve being rejected? Did they make you suffer so much?

***

VICTORIA

(*To KEVIN*) Did we make him suffer?

KEVIN

I don't think so. (*Pauses*) Perhaps some benign neglect.

VICTORIA

Benign neglect?

KEVIN

It just means we were busy with our own lives and let the kids grow up by themselves. Not that it really did them any harm.

VICTORIA

I never neglected our children! How could you even suggest such a thing?

KEVIN

No, not like that. They had clean clothes, good food and a nice house to live in (*swings his arms around*). But some children need more than that. Some need constant direction and attention.

VICTORIA

Oh poppycock! They got plenty of attention, as much as a busy mother of four could offer. (*Pauses*) Yes, I indulged in my arts and crafts, but we also played with them as kids, took them to movies and Disneyworld four times. We followed their schoolwork and did homework with them when they fell behind. (*Pauses*) There's no neglect there. No adverse childhood events as they call them these days. No sexual or psychological abuse. (*Pauses*) No, there was no neglect at all!

BY THE LETTER

KEVIN

Maybe just benign neglect.

VICTORIA

Whatever!

***

WANDA

(*To JACOB*) I bet you've already got your eye on another place around here, don't you?

JACOB

None of your business.

WANDA

Yes, it is, especially if there's no way we're going to keep the home place, not even visiting it as guests.

HEATHER

Fat chance! (*To WANDA*) He's willing to take a significant financial shellacking with the property taxes so he doesn't have to deal with us. Isn't that clear. (*To JACOB*) Isn't it true?

JACOB

Yes, it's true.

WANDA

And do you have another place in mind already? (*Pauses*) Do you?

JACOB

Yes, I do.

WANDA

On the lake or not?

JACOB

No, it's a bit inland.

WANDA

What's the address?

JACOB

None of your goddamned business!

WANDA

Why not? We could look it up on the Internet. Check out the price. Or drive by and take a peek. Furnished? Unfurnished? I'd be curious to see it? What did it cost, anyway?

HEATHER

(*To WANDA*) Lay off! He's not interested in us or what we think. And he's not interested in us knowing anything about his plans. (*Pauses*) It's probably furnished, that's why he didn't want any of the furniture. (*Pauses and looks around*) I loved this house, its location, the mountains, the lake, the hiking, the skiing and the backyard barbecues in the cold evening air. I liked the long happy hours talking with Mom and Dad. (*Pauses*) I could have lived without their conservative political views, but their humor and their sheer friendliness made up for it. This was a little bit of paradise in this mountain setting.

***

VICTORIA

See, she thought it was paradise, not hell. She enjoyed our company and the location and everything. (*Pauses*) She never exactly said it at the time, but you could tell she liked to come and visit and stay a week in the summer and a week in the winter for years and years.

KEVIN

You're right.

BY THE LETTER

VICTORIA

And it's almost all gone. All swept away with time and age and illness. First you, then me, and now this place. What a long, sad story of loss.

KEVIN

(*Shrugs*) I died pretty fast, but you hung on until you didn't even know your own children's names, much less this place. (*Pauses*) That was really sad.

VICTORIA

But I did remember. I couldn't express myself, but I would look at the picture of you and this place on the wall of the nursing home. Daniel painted it so I would see you and this house even if I couldn't really say it was you. (*Pauses*) It was well done and very comforting. (*Pauses*) Not sure what happened to that picture either.

KEVIN

It was very nice, a good likeness of me. (*Pauses*) All the kids came to visit you when they could. Jacob and Wanda came several times a week. (*Pauses*) I died fast, way too fast. There was no one there when I died and the girls really felt guilty, especially Wanda. She's always been kind hearted. (*Pauses*) Maybe that's why the girls want to hold on to this place, like holding on to a bit of us. Maybe it helps with their guilt, if they have any.

VICTORIA

And their brother won't let them hold on to it. I guess he doesn't have any guilt.

KEVIN

He shouldered a lot of the burden. Maybe that's what makes him angry and bitter or just tired. Maybe he forgot all the good times after he had to take care of all the bad times: paying taxes, paying bills, getting sitters, doing the yard work.

VICTORIA

Maybe. And maybe it's something else.

***

JACOB

(*To HEATHER*): If you like this area so much, you can just rent a condo or get a timeshare if you're that interested. The mountains will still be here and the lake and the hiking trails. You can get all of the benefits with none of the inconveniences.

WANDA

Maybe Heather can do that, but we sure can't and you know it. We can barely afford our rent, much less a week's vacation in the mountains in a timeshare. A third of the inheritance will barely cover our debts. (*Pauses*) I loved this place, too, mostly because of the good times with Mom and Dad. There were an amazing, funny and generous couple.

***

VICTORIA

Isn't that sweet?

KEVIN

Yes, very nice. Sounds a bit corny to me. Maybe she knows we're listening.

VICTORIA

You can be so cynical sometimes.

KEVIN

No, just realistic.

***

JACOB

They're dead and I'm the executor of the estate and I've made up my mind. There's nothing you can do about it. This place goes up for sale and Sophia and I are buying something new, with no strings attached and no emotional baggage.

HEATHER:
And Sophia agrees with this plan? Or did she think it up?

JACOB
Leave her out of this!

HEATHER
Just curious. Sophia and I are getting along much better now.

JACOB
Too curious.

WANDA
And what about all the contents? What about all this stuff (*gestures around the room.*)

JACOB
What about it?

WANDA
Can we pick some things we want to keep before the estate sale?

JACOB
What do you want exactly?

WANDA
I'd like the stained-glass window Mom made, and the big copper pot from Grandma, and the landscapes Mom did, at least one of them, if that's all right? I'd also like some of Daniel's paintings. They had a great collection of his work.

JACOB
Don't remind me!

HEATHER
And I'd like the ship model Dad made, and the mosaic table Mom made and one of those landscapes she did of this area. I'd like a couple of Daniel's paintings, too. (*To WANDA*) Maybe we can draw lots? You take some and I take the others. They're all beautiful paintings, Mom's and Daniel's. He inherited all the artistic talent, I guess. It was in his genes.

JACOB
Spare me. I don't want to talk about Daniel or his genes.

WANDA
(*To HEATHER*) Okay, that sound's fair. We'll draw lots. (*To JACOB*) Does any of this interest you? After all, they're Mom and Dad's handiwork. And those are your brother's paintings. That makes them all special.

JACOB
Take it all! I don't want anything by Mom or Daniel or even Dad. I'll remember them in my own way. I want a clean slate, a clean start and a free vision with no schmaltzy romantic overtones.

HEATHER
Schmaltzy romantic overtones? That's harsh. You never got along with Daniel, but his art was really very good. Some of his paintings are truly beautiful.

JACOB
NO! Especially not his paintings! They worshiped Daniel, at least Mom did. They made a museum to him in this place and it always bothered me. It still does. Take it all or I'll sell it or give it away. We can put it all in a garage sale or the garbage. I don't care, but I don't want to see any of it every again, especially Daniel's things. A new year and a new start! That's what I want.

BY THE LETTER

HEATHER
You never reconciled with Daniel or his death, did you?

JACOB
Don't bring that up now or every again. It's not reconciliation, it's disgust. Don't even mention his name. (*Pauses*) And this place and those paintings just bring up those same unpleasant memories. I want to bury them all in the deepest recesses of my mind.

HEATHER
Like burying Barbie?

JACOB
What's that supposed to mean?

HEATHER
Nothing, just an inside joke I had with Daniel. (*Pauses*) By the way, are any of those memories of him guilty ones, perhaps?

JACOB
No, just miserable ones.

WANDA
Were you so unhappy here? With everything?

JACOB
We had some good times here in this house, but it hasn't been fun taking care of everything after Dad died. Being executor is no joke; it's lots of work. (*Pauses*) And it hasn't been fun living in the shadow of clever, sociable and successful siblings (*looks at HEATHER*). Well, at least two of you were successful.

WANDA
Which two, Daniel and Heather? Thanks a lot! I know you think I'm a loser, you always have. And yourself, of course, another successful one.

JACOB
I was a Senior Vice President, damn it. What more could I have done?

WANDA
Yeah, at the company Dad helped create and where he sat on the board. What a coincidence.

JACOB
Shut up! That's a cheap shot. Dad may have helped me get my foot in the door, but I got to be a vice president by my own merits.

***

KEVIN
That's true, but he's always been very sensitive about it. And the girls just won't let it go. Daniel wouldn't either. I wonder if that's why Jacob killed him?

VICTORIA
Who knows exactly why? Such a sad story. Daniel could be annoying, but he didn't deserve to die. (*Pauses*) Jacob will have to live with that for the rest of his life, and beyond. Accident, indeed! (*Pauses*) Jacob's a clever boy, very articulate and intelligent. He would've succeeded anywhere with or without your help. It just so happened that he started at a place where you were on the founding board of directors. No one can hold that against him, can they?

KEVIN
I had some influence, of course, but Jacob climbed the corporate ladder all on his own. I wish Jacob would have full confidence in his own abilities. Sometimes I worry about that underlying insecurity.

VICTORIA
Don't worry too much. None of them lacks self-confidence. Daniel certainly didn't. I think they got that from you. You're smart and pretty

much self-made, from the bottom up, pulled yourself up by your own bootstraps.

KEVIN
Yeah, but the GI Bill gave me the boots and not everyone's that lucky these days. No one's completely self-made. Not in this world.

***

HEATHER
(*To JACOB*) So, what difference does that make? What's the big deal with being a vice president? Who cares?

JACOB
Mom and Dad loved you both, with all of your failings and issues, but never really acknowledged me as vice president of a multi-billion-dollar corporation. Doesn't that count, too? Isn't that worth some recognition, even more than for you two?

WANDA
Ah, that's it, you didn't get enough love and recognition from Mom and Dad, eh?

JACOB
And you caused them nothing but grief. You sucked the tit of their generosity until they wept from the pain. And that deserves unconditional love?

HEATHER
That's what parents do isn't it? Unconditional love?

JACOB
And you and your lesbian lifestyle. They suffered with that, too. You just couldn't lead a normal life with a husband and children, could you?

WANDA
You're a mean-spirited bigot. I can't have been easy for Mom and Dad or Heather, either, for that matter.

***

VICTORIA
He shouldn't hold that against Heather. We were shocked at first, but we got used to it, didn't we?

KEVIN
Yes, we did. Times changed and we did, too. He's wrong to bring that up. He's smart, but he can be tactless and insensitive.

***

HEATHER
(*To JACOB*) And a gingerbread house in the suburbs with a picket fence and all-white neighbors in a good school district. (*Pauses*) No, thank you!

WANDA
We had a child in a good school district and no picket fence. Nothing wrong with that.

JACOB
(*To WANDA*) And so did we, but they were adopted, somehow second-class grandkids compared to the "real" ones. That's what you always thought, isn't it?

WANDA
I never said that and I never heard Mom and Day say anything like that. Never!

***

BY THE LETTER

VICTORIA
She's right! We loved all of our grandchildren with the same degree of affection, the same thoughtfulness, and the same attention. Where's that ridiculous accusation coming from? Is he just paranoid?

KEVIN
Calm down. He's talking nonsense. He's upset and so are you.

VICTORIA
I'm upset, eh? What of it? Are you afraid that getting upset is going to give me a heart attack and kill me? Too late for that!

***

HEATHER
That's not true! Mom and Dad loved all the grandkids the same way and you know it. That's mean-spirited and insulting.

***

VICTORIA
Thanks, girl! (*To KEVIN*) I always loved her spunk, if not her lifestyle choice.

KEVIN
(*Stares at VICTORIA*) Can't imagine where she got that spunk from?

***

WANDA
(*To JACOB*) And they loved us all the same, too, with all of your successes and my failings. Can't you do the same with us? A little charity, for God's sake.

JACOB
God has nothing to do with it. And I don't have to love or respect either of you. So, live with it! I'm your brother, not your father. (*Pauses*) And

Mom and Dad had the good sense to make me executor of their estate, so live with that, too! At least they knew I would be fiscally responsible.

WANDA

(*To HEATHER*) Come on. This discussion is over; let's get out of here. (*Looks around the room*) Mom and Dad loved this place, they loved us and they loved all of their grandchildren. They enjoyed this house for decades and it's not going to be the home place anymore, ever. (*To JACOB*) Thanks for making things clear. Say hello to Sophia.

JACOB

Leave her out of this!

WANDA

Of course, but maybe she wouldn't mind be included.

JACOB

What's that supposed to mean?

WANDA

(*To JACOB*) Nothing, just say hello. (*To HEATHER*) Let's get out of here. We can pick these things up later. Maybe we can go out to lunch at that restaurant Mom and Dad always liked. It would be nice to catch up a little bit. We hardly even know one another.

HEATHER

I'd like that very much. We can come back tomorrow.

JACOB

Don't bother coming here ever again. I'll have everything you want shipped to you directly, at the estate's expense, of course.

HEATHER

Of course.

HEATHER and WANDA exit.

BY THE LETTER

JACOB
(*Sighs*) That went about as well as could be expected. (*Looks at the door*) Good riddance! (*Exits without looking back, slams the door.*)

***

> *VICTORIA and KEVIN are left alone in the room. They wander around and look at some of the articles.*

VICTORIA
Beautiful artwork. Don't you think? I hope it goes to good homes.

KEVIN
Yes, beautiful work. You were always the one with artistic sensibility, and Daniel, too. He definitely got that from you. (*Pauses*) I never expected him to die before we did. (*Shakes his head*) What a tragedy. (*Pauses*) He went too early and I guess now it's time for us to go, too. Give me your hand.

VICTORIA
(*Gives her hand to KEVIN*) Thanks for loving me. I really didn't always deserve it.

KEVIN
Nor did I. But I guess that's what unconditional love is all about, isn't it?

VICTORIA
(*Reaches over and kisses KEVIN*) Yes, unconditional love. (*Looks around a last time*) Let's go.

> *VICTORIA and KEVIN slowly exit together, hand in hand. "A Bridge over Troubled Waters" by Simon and Garfunkel or some other appropriate music plays softly.*

BLACKOUT

WORLD WAR II REMEMBRANCES OF KENNETH G. HOLCOMBE AND VIRGINIA HARVEY HOLCOMBE

SOME RECOLLECTIONS OF WORLD WAR II EXPERIENCES

By Kenneth Grant Holcombe

Having spent a year and a half at the University of California at Berkeley from January 1940 to May of 1941, I decided I had enough of mining engineering and enlisted in the U.S. Army on a one-year hitch to be assigned to the West Point Prep school at Fort Scott at the presidio at San Francisco. I had already expressed an interest in West Point and had made application to our Senator Knowland from California. The prep school was another avenue.

After three months in the Army, I began to question my resolve for four years at West Point and a career in the Army. Youthful indecisiveness was again about to change my life profoundly. Nowhere in my crystal ball did I see a war coming. As luck would have it, I saw a bulletin in the post exchange advertising the U.S. Maritime Commission and the Navy for a career at sea and an education as a cadet-midshipman at the U.S. Merchant Marine Academy in New York. The Army discharged me to the Maritime Commission and I began a new adventure, reporting to cadet school at the Navy base on Treasure Island in San Francisco Bay.

After a short three months at prelim school, another cadet, Neil Farley, short for Cornelius George Patrick Farley, of San Francisco and I were ordered to report to the U.S. Army Transport Willard A. Holbrook at Pier 49, Fort Mason, San Francisco. The ship was loading troops, the 147th and 148th National Guard Field Artillery Regiments, bound for the Philippines. We sailed the next day, November 22, 1941, for Pearl

Harbor, our first stop on what was to have been a round trip of perhaps 30 days duration. Little did we know! Our "peace time" troop rotation and our cargo also included crated P-40 fighter planes and 100 newly graduated army pilots from Randolph Field, Texas.

Our first stop was Pearl Harbor T.H. on November 28, 1941. On December 1, 1941, we set sail for the Philippines from this Navy base, soon to be devastated by the cowardly air attack of the Japs. We rendezvoused with eight other army and navy vessels and our convoy was escorted by the U.S.S. Pensacola, a heavy cruiser.

Six days later when the Japs attacked Pearl Harbor, you can imagine our concern for our situation. We gave as many paint brushes and as much paint of any color to the soldiers and painted the Holbrook, which was white, a very imaginative camouflage that was ugly, but reassuring.

The cruiser Pensacola, which carried very old catapult float planes, fired off a search plane, but the catapult misfired and the plane crashed into the sea. The pilot was rescued, the plane sank, and so much for our air search. Believe it or not, that pilot turned up in my dental class in San Francisco in 1947, and was none other than Tom Moore, who graduated with me in 1951. He said that dunking probably saved his life. His orders were to locate the Jap task force, three hundred and fifty fighters, bombers, etc., and report its location. That was a tall order. As it turned out, they were over 2,500 miles away. His plane had a maximum speed of 80 knots and a range of 500 miles. The Jap planes had speeds of 350 knots. The fortunes of war!

Our convoy began zig-zagging night and day and finally reached Suva, Fiji Island on December 13, 1941. The troops having been cooped up on the two transports were now bivouacked in the center of the Ascot Race Track until after Christmas. They were happy to get off the ship for any reason even though they were going to face Australia's hot and humid summer weather and what might lie ahead in the Philippines.

BY THE LETTER

The Holbrook sailed north from Brisbane on December 28, 1941, heading in the direction of the Philippines with most of the convoy arriving on January 6, 1941 in Darwin, Australia, the northernmost town on the continent and the most remote as well. From there, some of the convoy attempted to continue on to the Philippines, but were turned back by the overwhelming Jap Airforce. We suffered the loss of two of our ships at the battle of Timor in the Dutch East Indies. The badly battered convoy limped back to Darwin where the surviving troops disembarked. The Holbrook sailed with escort to Brisbane carrying evacuating families and wounded troops from the Philippines to safety.

In Melbourne, we added to our 600 air corps technicians with another 2,000 air corps personnel and additional fighter planes in the holds, this time crated and with all the parts and headed around southern Australia for Perth, where we arrived on February 18, 1942. We sailed from Perth in the company of the old U.S. carrier Langley, who had a deck load of assembled P-40s, the Sea Witch and the cruiser, Phoenix. As we proceeded north and east in the Indian Ocean, three days out, the Phoenix, Langley and Sea Witch left us, heading north toward Darwin. We were now escorted by the H.M.S. Enterprise, a British cruiser, as we headed toward India! We arrived March 6, 1942 at Colombo, Ceylon, and anchored in the outer harbor with many warships and merchant vessels.

We sailed March 7, 1942 from Colombo after being refueled and loaded with much needed drinking water, 2,000 plus troops use a lot and it was very hot. We headed north and west toward India. Our escorts were a British corvette and a Q ship converted raider, also British. We entered the Arabian Ocean still heading north and the corvette Hollyhock turned back to Colombo. We continued north through the Gulf of Carpentaria, heading for Karachi, India, perhaps. We heard some unconfirmed rumor that the Sea Witch and the Langley were both sunk by Jap planes off of Broome, Australia. We hoped not, but sadly, it was later confirmed.

One of the soldiers that boarded in Melbourne had a picture of the Pearl Harbor damage, our first look at the actual results of the air raid. Our escort and the Katooba dropped off to Bombay and we continued to Karachi, India, arriving March 12, 1942. We were carrying what would be the beginning of the 8th Air Force who flew what was to be called the "hump" and the back door to Jap forces holding the Dutch East Indies and the Malay Peninsula, including ill-fated Singapore. We sailed from Karachi the morning of March 28, 1942 after an interesting stay. We had short time and a chance to observe the primitive society unlike any I had seen. Some of the customs, both religious and social, took some getting used to.

We arrived in Bombay two days later on March 30, 1942 and, having been given both cholera and typhoid shots before arriving, I didn't feel at all well. We went in and immediately loaded over 2,000 Australian troops and nurses. They were returning home after suffering at the hands of Field Marshall Rommel's divisions in North Africa, Crete and Palestine. Many were wounded. The Katoomba and the Duntroon were already loading Aussie troops. On April 4, 1942, the Holbrook sailed from Bombay for Australia or so we thought. Wrong! The Japs bombed Colombo with carrier planes, wreaking destruction on the shipping, and yet we were sent into Colombo after the raid because they couldn't protect us at sea from carrier planes at any distance from land.

On April 8, 1942, we had sailed into Colombo. After loading water and witnessing the damage, we sailed out on April 12, 1942 with the Katoomba and Duntroon and escorts for Australia supposedly. Don't believe it! We turned westward towards Africa. Sure enough, our course seemed to be for East Africa and perhaps Mombasa, Kenya. On April 15, 1942, Duntroon, Holbrook and the merchant cruiser escort turned off for Mombasa while the Katoomba and her escort continued on toward Durban, South Africa. Needless to say, we did have some very unhappy passengers, the Aussies, who wanted to go home and so did we for that matter.

This world cruise was not scheduled this way. On April 20, 1942, after having been chased by a Vichy French submarine from Madagascar, the convoy pulled into the harbor of Mombasa where three old time battleships of the British Navy lay at anchor, the Ramales, Resolution and Royal Sovereign, hiding out from the German pocket battleships, Bismarck, Graff Spree, etc. who roamed the Indian Ocean. There were many British naval vessels. Mombasa seemed a haven in the war and the Aussie troops were let ashore for a few hours for some much-needed R & R. We sailed the next day for Durban and expected to get there in five days. Mombasa was an interesting and unexpected diversion and I would have liked to have had more time there.

We arrived at Durban on the morning of April 27, 1942, a beautiful and very modern city on the Indian Ocean on the East Coast of South Africa. There was a lively and hospitable social scene and no blackouts, it seemed, aside from the from the fact that the city was certainly on a full war-time footing. Never have I seen so many varied uniforms of the world's military establishments. On May 1, 1942, we sailed in convoy for Australia to cross the Indian Ocean to Perth, distance of 4,500 miles which took 15 days and required water rationing for the same Australian troops and nurses we picked up in Bombay, a frustrated and exhausted group, but real troopers and just delighted to finally be on their way home. We, too, hopefully.

The Holbrook sailed into Fremantle, the port for Perth, on the evening of May 14, 1942, after a long and rough trip in some stormy seas on the Indian Ocean, wintertime south of the equator maybe a little like the North Atlantic. We departed Fremantle on May 17, 1942 for Adelaide with the Aussie troops still aboard. They were to disembark in our next port, Adelaide, rather than Perth, and we had some very disappointed troops. They had been aboard a long time and away from home fighting a war with the Germans for two years already. On May 22, 1942, we sailed into Adelaide after a few rough and really turbulent seas, enough to tear off some of the port bow rail and carry away one of the large life rafts. The soldiers were to parade in review for General Bennett, who had been evacuated from Singapore when 17,000 Australian troops were captured by the Japs. When we tied up at the dock, the troops had other ideas and they just walked away, dropping their Bren guns and apparently heading home. Quite a sight, and I never heard the outcome. They were not happy with Bennett. Guess our General McArthur of Philippine fame, "I shall return," was lucky.

Our return to the States began to look promising. On May 28, 1942, we departed Adelaide, bound for Sydney. The ship hugged the coast and encountered traffic in both directions. This tactic served two purposes. With no escorts available, we were a less attractive target for enemy submarines near the coast, while air cover was frequent and on call. The weather was treacherous, but also afforded cover and hindered submarines as well. We pulled into Sydney Harbor on May 30, 1942, Memorial Day in the U.S., passing the U.S.S. Chicago and several of our destroyers. Sydney is a large and modern city, not unlike many in the States. By this time, of course, it was loaded with U.S. servicemen serving in all areas of the South Pacific, etc.

While we were in the Sydney Harbor, it seems three midget Jap subs snuck in around the nets and torpedoed a ferry boat, of all things, while we were at anchor in the harbor and an easy target, but remained unharmed. This has been a lucky ship. Imagine torpedoing a ferry boat with the harbor full of military ships and every imaginable war cargo ship.

We sailed for home on June 2, 1942 after loading six thousand tons of wool, and many merchant crewmen who lost their ships to enemy action and needed a ride home. There were also many families with children, perhaps sixty. We had a bad start. The wind was severe and the ship didn't answer the helm. It got worse and we lost an anchor with 60 fathoms of chain. Dropped the other one and sailed until dawn when the wind subsided. Not a good start for the many civilians on a troop ship, and by this time the Holbrook was beginning to look shabby and in need of a ship yard. I had done my best to paint most of the ship single handed, 22 life boats and ten big rafts, all of the troop latrines, and still manage to stand watches on the bridge at sea and learn navigation, ship handling and cargo stowage, etc. I'm not sure how well I did with a chief mate who was certainly not in sympathy with the cadet system and didn't make it easy.

BY THE LETTER

We took a detour stopping off at Wellington, New Zealand. Incidentally, there were five Navy transports in the harbor, including a sister ship to the Holbrook, the former Army transport American Legion. We arrived in Wellington on June 7, 1942 and left for home on the 8th. This navy task force probably was the Guadalcanal invasion force. On June 25, 1942, (216 days later), we sailed through the Golden Gate into San Francisco Bay after having been gone seven months and three days, over 40,000 miles through hostile waters in many oceans and returned home without a scratch. A trip I will never forget nor will my folks who had little news of me because the circumstances didn't allow it. What a way to enter WW II!

After a wonderful few days at home with my folks and catching up on what all had happened to the rest of the world during these months, I reported to the U.S. Merchant Marine Academy at Kings Point, New York, to complete my training. I graduated with the class of A103 in February, 1943. Upon graduation, I received my third mates license and commission as ensign in the U.S. Naval Reserve along with a set of Navy orders to active duty, a short tour as an instructor back at the Academy as it turned out.

After a short time at Kings Point, I was ordered to report to the amphibious attack cargo ship, the U.S.S. Bellatrix, AKA 3, at Charleston Navy Yard in South Carolina. I was assigned as a deck watch officer and small boat officer to ride in with the tank lighters during the invasions. We carried on our decks both troop carriers LCVPs (landing craft, vehicle, personnel) and tank carriers LCMs (landing craft mechanized). We did carry the Sherman tanks and their crews, but the LCVPs after launching were loaded with troops from the accompanying transports. We sailed in whatever the opposition on the beach or the ocean conditions. Neither the Japs nor the Germans gave any quarter.

We made two such landings while I was aboard, the invasion of Sicily in the Mediterranean Theatre and the Island of Tarawa in the Gilbert Islands in the South Pacific. Sicily was in June of 1943 (an army invasion from North Africa) and Tarawa in November 1943 (a marine amphibious force).

Immediately after Tarawa, I received orders to New London, Connecticut to submarine school for which I had applied many months back. I flew home from what was called Sowestpac (South West Pacific) by the Navy to a December winter in New London, that was a change in weather from ninety degrees to subzero. With sufficient antifreeze and some midnight oil, the class graduated in ninety days and my orders read to report to Midway Island and further assignment to a submarine. After a small detour with my roommate, Bob Kennedy, to his home in Palatka, Florida, we hitched a ride on a Navy plane to California. We bought a car to drive west, but it only made it 50 miles before breaking down and if recollection serves me, we gave it away and hitched a ride on a Navy plan from Jacksonville. My dad did, however, certainly appreciated the ration tickets for gasoline and tires that we gave him.

From the relief pool at Midway, I was assigned to the U.S.S. Gar SS 206, an older boat built in 1940. She was short one officer in her crew. There had been an aborted duty assignment a few days earlier when I reported aboard the Herring SS 233 at Midway as she was topping off fuel after leaving Midway. The captain wanted an officer with more engineering experience than I had and asked me if there were others in the pool who might fit the bill. He found one. I never even unpacked and went back up to the BOQ. The Herring was reported lost on that patrol. I have been on lucky ships and it continued, serving unscathed aboard the Gar for her last three successful war patrols.

After those patrols on the Gar, we finished the last few months of the war at Ulithi and Saipan as a training target vessel for anti-submarine vessels and aircraft. The Gar had refits in Majuro, Brisbane, Australia and Pearl Harbor during those 1944-1945 years.

Certainly, the highlight of my wartime years was meeting my future wife, Virginia, in Australia. We both were doing a little R & R at Surfers Paradise in Southport, Australia. It was and still is the jewel of

BY THE LETTER

Queensland State, the gold coast of Australia, then a barren and beautiful beach with a couple of two-story wooden hotels and even camels on the beach, offspring of the camels imported from India when they built the railroad across the continent. Virginia was a U.S. Navy nurse stationed in Brisbane, the best-looking gal I had ever seen and nicknamed Miss Sunshine by her patients and colleagues. How can you do any better than that? She was a real keeper. It was only November of 1944 and who knew when we would meet again. Her duty station was the U.S. Naval Hospital MOB 109 in Brisbane.

The Gar went north to supply the Philippine guerrillas on Luzon and made several trips with ammunition, medical supplies, guns, radios, etc. and rescued downed pilots, and delivered secret military papers for General MacArthur prior to the U.S. return to the Philippines. Virginia, meanwhile, was receiving orders to Oak Knoll Naval Hospital in Oakland, California.

The Gar was ordered back to Pearl Harbor after our next patrol for an overhaul in the navy yard. What fantastic timing! And with a little help from the Navy, Virginia was able to stop over in Hawaii where we arranged a spectacular wedding at the submarine base chapel. Our new skipper, Murray Frazee, lately of the ill-fatted submarine Tang SS 306, was my best man. All the officers pitched in to help with our wedding and reception plans. The wedding was at the sub base chapel and the reception was at the officer's club at the sub base with the Ray Anthony Navy Band for dancing. Virginia even had two Navy nurse bride maids she knew stationed locally who were delighted to participate. The Navy chaplain was also from the base so it was an all-around Navy affair. Virginia was given away by Capt. O'Reagan, a submarine squadron Commander. We even had a three-week honeymoon in Honolulu, courtesy of the Navy, after which Virginia went on to Oakland. The Gar completed overhaul, sailed to Saipan and Ulithi until the end of the war. Virginia was discharged as married nurses were not allowed to remain in the service at the time.

I was transferred to the sub tender Orion for prize duty in Japan at war's end to help bring a Jap sub home, if you can believe that. However, with more than enough time in service, I rode the tender back to New York, met Virginia and we headed home. The finale for both of us from the Navy, for which we shared kind feelings and a sense of pride, was to be aboard the submarine tender, Orion, anchored in the Hudson River off New York City on Navy Day, November 27, 1945, with a portion of the fleet that was reviewed by President Harry Truman from the destroyer Renshaw.

It was a fitting end for our participation in World War II and the beginning of our new life together. I was discharged and we headed home to California by train. Virginia's sister, Elinor, was able to come from Cleveland, Ohio, to be with us on the sub tender for the final Navy salute to the sailors by the President, and ours to him for having the courage to end this long and costly war so decisively.

Campaign ribbon and awards of World War II:

Asiatic-Pacific campaign 1941-1945 Navy Battle Star, Tarawa Invasion
European-African-Middle Easter theatre 1941-1945 Navy Battle Star, Sicily Invasion
Victory medal WWII Navy
Victory medal merchant Marine WWII
Philippine Liberation medal 1941-1945
Philippine Independence medal
Merchant Marine Pacific zone WWII
Merchant Marine defense medal WWII
Submarine Patrol combat pin, Navy, plus two additional gold stars
Philippine Presidential Unit Citation – U.S. Submarine Gar – Guerilla support patrols 1944

VIRGINIA'S HISTORY

By Virginia Ruth Holcombe (née Harvey)

I was born in Ohio in 1920. My father died when I was seven and my six-year old sister and I were raised by a loving mother and our maternal grandparents. We moved to Louisville Kentucky, in 1934 and afterwards moved back to Ohio. I graduated from high school in Lancaster, Ohio, and entered nurses training at Lancaster Hospital. After graduation, I worked at my hospital and then at Children's Hospital in Columbus Ohio from 1941 until November of 1942. I then joined the U.S. Navy Nurse Corps and received orders to report to the U.S. Navy Hospital in San Diego, California.

One year later, orders arrived to board the U.S.S. Point, formerly the S.S. America, now converted to carry eight thousand troops. We sailed from San Francisco on November 24, 1943 and seventeen days later (December 10, 1943), we anchored in Milne Bay, New Guinea. We transferred to the H.M.S. Katoomba for the last leg of our voyage to Townsville, Australia, another three days. A flight from there and we arrived at what became U.S. Naval Hospital #9, which had just been built by C.B.s in Brisbane, Australia.

For the net fourteen months, I cared for terrific patients, met wonderful Australians, superb co-workers and my future husband, Ken. Ken's ship, the U.S.S. Gar was in for a refit at the submarine base in Brisbane and we met on an R & R weekend at Surfers Paradise. We met again the following year and were married in Pearl Harbor at the submarine base on January 20, 1945 with all Navy attendants and guests. I returned to the States and met his wonderful parents, Jerry and Ardine ("Pet") Holcombe, and together we waited for the war to end. Eight months later, Ken arrived home.

His mom and dad said they had partied all afternoon the day of our wedding as they weren't sure when it was two p.m. in Hawaii. My mother said she had reread all my old letters to see if I had ever mentioned Ken's name (and said she had never found it!)

Four years of dental school followed. We became parents of Jerry, David and Holly and bought a house. Wendy arrived in 1957 and we bought a bigger house in Walnut Creek, California, where we have lived ever since. Ken practiced dentistry four years with his dad in Oakland and then opened his own office in Lafayette, California. He retired after thirty-five years in 1985. He was active in Kiwanis and all dental activities. I joined the Jr. Alliance and held several offices in the Dental Auxiliary, becoming president in 1957. Being a mother filled all the other spaces.

TWO SHORT STORIES

ROCK AND A HARD PLACE

My name is Claudia Gomez-Gonzalez and I come from a small village in the mountains of Guatemala. We lived there, my two children and me, with my *abuela*, my grandmother on my mother's side. Our village sits on a hillside, surrounded by lush jungle, filled with flowering plants and tropical birds, a real paradise. Nothing, however, masks our grinding poverty. *Abuela* and I sold tortillas on the plaza, but we even had to give some of that money to the gangs. Our tiny garden helped, and then the hurricanes came and washed everything away.

My husband long since left for *el norte* and disappeared into the vastness of that land without ever reaching out to us. I have an uncle in Chicago who sometimes sends a few dollars to the *abuela*, but not enough to live on. When I decided to make the trip to *el norte* myself, *abuela* refused. She watched her husband and her sons go there and never return. She did not know whether they were alive or dead, yet she prayed each night to the Holy Virgin as she recited the rosary. Yet, in the end, even she knew we had no choice, I had to make the trip.

We sold the little land she still possessed and I paid a coyote to get me safely to *el norte*. In Mexico we confronted every danger: thieves, kidnappers, rapists, drug gangs and constant heat, thirst and hunger. Sometimes crammed in the back of a stifling truck, I wanted to die. But the dream of *el norte* and a good job, with the hopes of money to send to my children and the *abuela* kept me going. Each night, I recited the rosary that *abuela* gave me before I left and I prayed that the Holy Virgin would see me through to the promised land.

BY THE LETTER

When we finally arrived at the border, the camp on the Mexican side looked and smelled like hell. Men, women and children were crammed together with almost no food, put plenty of garbage and excrement. And always the gangs hanging around to snatch the unwary or unprotected, selling children and women into slavery. Only our coyote kept us safe by paying them a part of the fee, the price for safety.

The night to cross arrived and the coyote gave us each an inner tube and told us just the right moment to get across between patrols. He explained the we were to separate and hide in the bushes to wait until dawn, then only come out when we saw a border agent with a badge. Vigilantes, who might kill us, also roamed the U.S. side, but an agent would take us in to be processed. If we qualified for asylum and had an address in the U.S., we might be sent there.

After crossing in the dark water, I moved into the dense brush and shivered with cold in my soaking clothes. Creatures moved around making it impossible to sleep. When dawn finally came, I heard the rumbling of trucks and voices in English. I peeked out from the bushes and saw a man, a tall white man, in a dark uniform with an American flag on his shoulder. He yelled something in my direction, but I did not understand. I wanted to show myself, but I felt paralyzed with fear. He yelled again. But I stayed still, wanting to go out, but too afraid.

When I saw the black snake near my ankle, I stood up and burst through the shrubbery. My dress got tangled in the bushes and I tried to yank it out. He yelled some more and finally I plunged forward toward him as if he were Christ himself. I only saw the glint of the gun as the bullet struck my head. I remembered hearing that you see your whole life pass in front of you in the seconds before you die. I saw my mama, my *abuela*, my children as babies and the beautiful green jungle dotted with multi-colored birds and flowers before falling backwards. I looked heavenward as I fell back and saw the glorious Holy Virgin, surrounded by flames like Our Lady of Guadalupe and I saw a trace of a smile on her lips as she extended her arms to take me to her bosom, far beyond *el norte* to the real promised land.

DEATH IN THE SUPERMARKET

My name is Laquitta Lewis and I'm a 41-year-old cashier at the local supermarket, the last one in our neighborhood. It's not a very good job, but at least it pays a little over minimum wage. My salary covers the rent and helps keep the kids and me in food and clothes with an occasional videogame on the side. I'd like to live in a better neighborhood, but most places require a hefty security deposit and they don't take Blacks anyway, especially a single mother. There's a lot of reasons to move: better schools, more parks, less guns and drugs. But if you don't have the money, what can you do? It's not legal to discriminate, everyone knows, but it still happens.

The boss here isn't a bad man. He's Pakistani or something, and his accent is sometimes hard to understand, but he keeps the supermarket open in this neighborhood. He employs a lot of locals like me, too. And if it wasn't for him and this place, it would just be those nasty corner stores with liquor, cigarettes and junk food.

When COVID came, we all had to wear masks. I really didn't want to work at all, but with kids at home and rent to pay, there was no way I could stop working and stay home, stimulus check or not. In the beginning, the customers were pretty good about wearing masks and staying apart. We had signs on the door that said "Masks Required," and I didn't think much of the whole thing until COVID really got started. My grandpa died, my auntie died, my uncle almost died and everybody started getting COVID right and left. My mother still lived in a nursing home and I couldn't go see her at all, just look at her through the window and cry.

BY THE LETTER

After that, I started taking this COVID thing real seriously. I wanted that vaccine bad, but it took forever to get to my age group. They started with the nursing homes, thank God, then the 70-year-olds and above, then 65 and older and finally they got down to my age group. I heard all the fussing about this and that with the vaccine, but there was no way I wasn't getting vaccinated. I waited hours in line in the rain twice to get my two shots and it was worth every minute.

The only problem was that they said we could get re-infected. I thought vaccination was the end of the story, but no, you could still get the damn COVID. So, when the boss says we've got to continue wearing masks that cover the nose and mouth, I agreed 100% without any objection. No way I was going to get the virus when I had already escaped. If people wanted to put their own lives at risk, so be it, but the boss also said we had to be the mask police. We had to tell customers to put on their masks and wear them right, covering the mouth and nose. So, I'm telling old ladies, young kids, policemen and teenagers to wear their masks right. That was a bore. People started to look at me like I was a prison warden and I heard all sorts of nasty remarks about being a mask Nazi. Just part of the job, I supposed.

Then this guy comes up with a mask under his nose and barely over his lips and plops his groceries at my register. I said politely, "Sir," I always use sir and ma'am because that's the way I was raised. "Sir, can you pull up your mask over your nose, please." Instead of just doing it, he drops his groceries on the conveyer belt and stomps out without paying. I pulled the items off the belt and put them to the side so the next customer can come through and I didn't see that same guy come back into the store. When I looked up, I could see he was angry as hell and he wasn't wearing a mask at all. His lips were twisted back in a snarl. I was staring so hard at his flashing eyes and crooked, yellow teeth that I didn't even see the gun in his hand as he shot me point blank in the chest.

They say you can see your whole life flash before your eyes before you die. I saw my grandma and my mother and my kids as I fell backwards onto the linoleum tiles. I looked up at the fluorescent lights as the ceiling opened up revealing the smiling face of Jesus, a Black person like me. I barely heard the gunshot of our security guard, Fred, that took down the killer before Jesus took me in his arms and lifted me out of the last supermarket in our Godforsaken, COVID-infested neighborhood.

ABOUT THE AUTHOR

David J. Holcombe was born in 1949 in San Francisco, California, and raised in the East Bay in Walnut Creek. He passed a tranquil youth and adolescence, riding to school on a bicycle through pear orchards that still lined the country roads. At Las Lomas High School, his English teacher introduced their Advanced English class to creative writing, something he pursued at U.C. Davis under the tutelage of Diane Murray-Johnson (author of "*Le Divorce*" and "*Le Mariage*.")

While always attracted to art, writing and dancing, the realities of life induced him to pursue a medical career, a path that lead him to the Catholic University of Louvain in Brussels, Belgium. His knowledge of four years of high school French allowed him to excel in medical school despite the rigor of the Belgian educational system. Returning to a residency at a Johns-Hopkins affiliated clinic in Baltimore, he and his wife and three sons then moved to Central Louisiana in 1986 where their fourth son was born.

There, in the middle of the rural South, he practiced medicine for twenty years while raising a family and resuming both painting and creative writing. After twenty years of internal medicine, he pivoted to public health and became the Regional Administrator/Medical Director of the Louisiana Office of Public Health for Central Louisiana. During his years in Alexandria, Louisiana, he self-published twelve books (all of them commercial flops) and saw a dozen of his short plays produced by Spectral Sisters Productions, a local developmental theatre group.

Science and art have co-existed in an uneasy balance during his entire life. He has been called too artsy to be a good doctor and too scientific to be a good artist. Being torn between these conflicting poles has provided much of the tension that fuels his artistic output. While his books remain unsold, his art has had some modest success in local-regional exhibits and has found its way into a number of collections, both here and abroad.

He hopes that his artistic output will be discovered by generations yet unborn as an expression of a true artistic spirit, stuck in a most unlikely environment. When he moved from Baltimore in 1986, the Residency Director learned of the proposed destination, Alexandria, Louisiana. He commented at the time that "you won't find any soul brothers there." Those prophetic words have remained with me for over 30 years. With much effort, however, there have been some gathering of kindred souls in Central Louisiana, leading me to believe that you can find like-minded spirits in even the most unlikely places.

www.ingramcontent.com/pod-product-compliance
Lightning Source LLC
Chambersburg PA
CBHW021423070526
44577CB00001B/27